To Dvora,
my love, my partner, and my spiritual leader

WHAT WILL YOU DRINK?

Quenching Thirst Through the Ages

ARIE L. MELNIK

Post Hill
PRESS

A POST HILL PRESS BOOK
ISBN: 978-1-64293-374-1
ISBN (eBook): 978-1-64293-375-8

What Will You Drink?
Quenching Thirst Through the Ages
© 2020 by Arie L. Melnik
All Rights Reserved

Cover art by Cody Corcoran
Author photo by Neta Fishman

Post Hill Press
New York • Nashville
posthillpress.com

Published in the United States of America

Thanks

As in any book of this kind, my work relies also on research of others. At the end of the book I placed a long list of sources that assisted me. I got help also from papers in periodicals and interviews. When writing this book, I used the advice of several knowledgeable persons; some are mentioned in the text, and others provided advice "behind the scenes." I am thankful to David Kroyanker, who has tremendous experience in writing books. Thanks are due to Renana Ravitsky Pilzer, who is always happy to answer questions on Jewish subjects. Special thanks I send to my old teacher Nachum Gross, who introduced me to the complexity of written history and showed me the path that leads to better understanding of events. On the development of the production of milk and distribution in the 1930s, I learned from Shalom Grol and Yossef Shalev, who shared with me their valuable personal knowledge. I also wish to thank Aya and Elisha Cohen, Michal Shalev, Nir Rachkovsky, and Eshkol Nevo, who read parts of the manuscript and told me how to improve it. An additional gratitude I owe to Oded Abramsky and Yael Nov, who encouraged me in the process of writing the manuscript and reminded me that it is a worthy project. I am in debt to Noam Lester, who diligently corrects linguistic errors and clarifies wrong sentences cheerfully. I also thank Chana Tyman-Levy, who made my English flow properly. Heartfelt thanks I owe to Adi Fishman, who helped in the writing process and cleared it of obvious mistakes. I am in debt to my agent, Lynne Rabinoff, who leads me in the turbulent water of publishing. I am also thankful to my publisher, Post Hill

Press, for guiding the publication and marketing process. Finally, special gratitude I owe to my wife, Dvora, for encouragement and support during the process of writing this book. I also thank my children, Ayelet, Ronen, and Barak, that my occupation in writing surrounds them in most of their lives.

Table of Contents

Chapter Six: Tea (and Rice) in China and India

Chapter Seven: Coffee, Wakefulness and Enlightenment

Chapter Eight: Soft Drinks

Preface

DRINKERS' PARADISE

There is no life without drinking something. Maybe this is why every social or business meeting starts with the question "Would you like something to drink?" Today, in the twenty-first century, we have a wide selection of beverages to choose from. Indeed, in a nearby supermarket I found no fewer than thirty-seven types of soft drinks in a variety of flavors, fourteen brands of beer, and thirty-one different wines, as well as seventeen brands of tea and thirteen of coffee. In other words, the variety of beverages offered to the public is quite impressive. However, this was not always the case. In the distant past, people drank only water. But over the last centuries, an increasing choice of beverages has become accessible to all social classes. This book tells the history of the beverages commonly consumed in a world that may be described as a drinkers' paradise.

For as long as I can remember, I have been interested in beverages. During my early adulthood, I became engrossed in the history of drinks and drinking habits. While in my twenties, I sought to enhance my experience and tasted almost every known beverage. Later on, I began gathering historical data as well as anecdotes about drinking and beverages. My fascination with the history of food and drink dates from the early 1960s, when I took classes in economic sciences under Professor Nachum Gross. Back then, historians turned their attention to researching everyday life in past centuries. Among the leaders of this trend was the French historian Fernand Braudel, from whom I learned a great deal in terms of interpreting documented history. But the turning point for me occurred when I visited major museums in Europe, where I had the opportunity to contemplate depictions of tables ready and set for meals. To me those paintings represented the very physical aspect of history, and already then, I wondered, *What beverages were served in those glasses and goblets in the reproduced scenes?*

I gained additional knowledge from exhibitions and palaces in France, Italy, Denmark, and other countries, where I could admire dinner tables set for princes and counts. Dining arrangements of the rich and famous are also exhibited in historical mansions in Newport, Rhode Island. Whenever I visited one such exhibition, I could not help wondering, *What was the content of those glasses and plates displayed on the table?* and I searched for any available documentation. From the rich and famous, I soon moved on to the less privileged social classes, and I investigated the consumption of food and drinks throughout society. This led to my further inquiry into the production of beverages, the interaction between manufacturers and politicians, and the technology of the relevant era.

The motivation for writing this book was my interest in the history of drinking and of the manufacture of beverages, and hence I embarked on this project from a historical point of view. The realm of food and drink is wide-ranging, and so I chose to focus solely on drinking. When I searched through the literature on beverages, I did not find a single book that provided a synthetic approach to the production and consumption of beverages as part of a wider scope of human activity. The majority of history books addresses the consumption of food and drinks merely as an anecdotal activity.

This book is about quenching thirst. The information contained in it, which I gathered from numerous books and scholarly articles, aims at describing the development of beverages and of drinking habits and their connection with other facets of life. This information is, in my humble view, of universal interest, even though it may digress from the reader's daily occupations.

This here is a rather uncommon history book, as books on history generally tend to disregard the topic of food and drink. It also differs from cookbooks, in that the latter mainly emphasize the technical aspects of creating food. While discussing the various beverages, this book strives to uncover the—sometimes hidden—ways in which they relate to social behavior, business activity, and politics.

Regarding bibliography, it should be noted that whereas we do have information on foods and beverages during the antiquity, little knowledge has reached us as far as the Middle Ages are concerned. The written history of beverages starts in the fourteenth century, thanks to a large amount of texts preserved from then onwards. There are hardly any earlier written records on this topic, and the only sources of information are medical texts and archaeological findings. Based on the sparse knowledge about the Middle Ages, we learn that the poor drank mainly water. Middle-class families could afford beer and wine, as well as better food, which they cooked themselves. Public eating facilities existed only in the form of roadhouses. We furthermore have some records, earlier than the twelfth century, of official feasts and celebrations, such as wedding meals or diplomatic occasions, but with hardly any details on the actual meal. Literary sources, as well, are highly reticent on the types of food served during the Middle Ages and merely mention the fact that celebrations were held.

Eating and drinking are simple acts performed on a daily basis, but when considering them from a historical point of view, they become complex and many-sided. We are not interested in the individual who drinks a beverage, but rather in the manner in which the individual's consumption of beverages associates with other behaviors, both at the individual and collective level. Thus, it is useful to examine the various beverages while outlining the limits of their impact. The approach illustrated in this book is to combine the detailed description of basic beverages (such as tea or coffee) with a discussion on their connection with social and public behaviors. Each of this book's chapters deals with one type of beverage and investigates how it influenced—and was influenced by—historical, sociological, political, and technological developments. Each discussion encompasses aspects of production as well as consumption of the relevant beverage throughout history.

Chapter One

ALL WHO ARE THIRSTY, COME TO THE WATERS

1. Ancient History

Just as with any economic product, water depends on capital investment to produce and transport it. So it comes at a price. In order to cover the cost of pumping and pipes, it has to be a significant price. There are opponents to this cost who say that drinking water is a basic right and that citizens should receive it almost free of charge. But if there is no one to pay for it, there will be no pipes or plumbing, and no water in our homes.

Indeed, it has always been a challenge to provide drinking water to the public, since fresh water has been a condition for the existence of any civilization since the beginning of time. Drinking water is both a physical resource and a necessity for physical existence. Failure to drink water in an arid zone means risking death. The problem is that it is a heavy resource that is difficult to package and deliver, and it is also difficult to keep the water clean and free of pollutants.

Because of the importance of drinking, ancient civilizations were already involved in irrigation and the diversion and transport of water, and water reservoirs have been found in archaeological excavations in many places in Asia and America. The Bible is full of references[1] to springs, wells, and streams, as well as to less

---

1   The name of the present chapter is a quote from Isaiah 55:1.

popular sources, as it is said in Nehemiah 9:15: "And You brought them water out of the rock for their thirst." Water is mentioned in the Bible as a public resource and that it belonged to everyone in its natural state. However, when there were transport and storage costs, people did not have open access, and a priority scale had to be established—that is, a ranking of uses. The first priority was usually given for drinking, and only afterwards for irrigation. In the drinking category, preference was generally given to the local dwellers, and only then was the right of use given to others.

This is also the Muslim approach. The Quran explicitly states that whoever gives water to every creature will be rewarded. Water is a gift from God, and everyone has the right to access it. The Muslim rule was adopted by the Ottoman Empire, which imposed the obligation to provide drinking water to its citizens and residents. Yet sometimes God Himself limits the amount of water available. When this occurred, believers also limited the amount of water each family could draw (free of charge) from a public well. It was usually twenty liters per family.

Still, the question arises: who is to make sure that water is available and how to finance it? Here we can learn from ancient Rome. The Romans established aqueducts for water transport (even in the middle of the nineteenth century, Karl Marx wrote of his admiration of them). The system of water supply and distribution in ancient Rome was very impressive. Over some five hundred years, eleven aqueducts were built in Rome, and the water was transported and distributed by force of gravity. The water was used not only for drinking, but also for bathing in the famous bathhouses. Within the city there were small neighborhood reservoirs (distribution centers) called *lacus*, from which most of the residents took water in buckets for domestic use free of charge.

During the reign of Emperor Augustus, these distribution centers numbered around six hundred. But there was also private demand for water for the city's wealthy. Some of the water carried by the aqueducts arrived at the distribution points, while another part (approximately 40 percent) was transported by pipes directly to the homes of the affluent residents who paid a "water tax." In other words, there was a cross-subsidy—part of the population paid, and some had a "natural right" to take water free of charge.

Construction of the aqueduct water transport system involved immense expense, and even after the construction itself, ongoing maintenance required additional resources. Therefore, the consumption of water was subject to payment, paid by the wealthy of Rome. Chroniclers have rightly argued that the great public works for water transport and the improvement of roads for traffic were also done to enhance the ruler's reputation and fame, and to remind the citizens who was concerned for their welfare. To this end, great decorated water fountains were built (especially in the time of Augustus, Tiberius, and Claudius). In practice, it was necessary to pay for this crucial commodity, and the payment was borne by the city's wealthy.

2. Water in Modern Times

Was the Roman custom accepted in later generations? Let's examine the history of drinking water in London and New York. The first residents of New York City (originally called New Amsterdam) were Dutch. They drew water from wells that were privately owned. After the British conquered the city in 1664, additional wells were drilled in the new neighborhoods, and the residents of the surrounding areas were asked to pay for the construction of the wells. They were also charged for the ongoing maintenance of the wells. Over time, the wells became polluted, and pure drinking water for cooking purposes—known as "tea water"—began to be sold to the discerning. After the US War of Independence, the quality of this cooking water also declined, and it was necessary to transport water to the city from farther sources. The New York City municipality approved a project, funded by taxes and loans, to build a pipeline system of nearly fifty kilometers by a company founded specifically for this purpose. Over the course of the nineteenth century, other public companies were established, also with public funds and loans, and each time, they needed to move farther north to draw water. The distances of water sources from the city led to an increase in expenditure, while public funding increased. Eventually public ownership of the water supply became the norm.

The London water system also underwent a similar process. During the Middle Ages, residents drew water from private wells for a fee or from the Thames River for free. Since the city's sewage also flowed into the Thames, the river water available to all was neither tasty nor healthy. The nobility drank spring water that was transported in tanks to the payer's home. In the sixteenth century, when the population grew significantly, the city of London still refused to finance a public water project for the city, and the supply of quality drinking water remained in private hands. Nine separate private water companies operated in London until the mid-nineteenth century. The cholera epidemic that broke out in the city in 1840, due to polluted water, caused the need for munic-ipal supervision of the water supply (incidentally, John Snow founded the science of epidemiology during this period). Only in the early twentieth century, or more precisely in 1902, was the Metropolitan Water Board established. Until then, philanthropic associations provided water to the poor through urban distribution points, which the wealthy public paid for.

In the cases of both London and New York, water supply began as a private enterprise, some of which was used for the benefit of the city's poor free of charge, but for the most part involved a fee. Later, both cities switched to a public-municipal system, and pricing methods had to be determined. This has been the case in other cities and in other countries as well, and the issue of financing and pricing of water is still contested in developed countries. In addition, it is important to remember that in the underdeveloped countries, basic sanitation conditions are lacking and pure drinking water is a long-term vision. More than two billion people in these countries must use brackish water, at a minimal price, and suffer from diseases associated with the use of polluted water.

3. Water and Disease

In the past, and even today, saturated water may at times spread disease. Even before a basic knowledge of bacteria and viruses, the public knew that water does not always carry good news. The Romans kept water as pure as possible in accordance with the technology of their time. The aqueducts and canals carried water long distances, and before it reached its destination, the water passed through settling pools, in which visible foreign matter was separated and removed. But this Roman technology was forgotten over the years, and in the Middle Ages—in London and Paris, for example—water was pumped directly from the river crossing the city even when it was common knowledge that sewage ran through open channels to the same river. City residents could draw water in buckets themselves or buy water from private suppliers who piped the water from the river to the customers' homes. In Paris, the number of paying customers was estimated at only four thousand people. For hundreds of years, few public bodies (governments and municipalities) have invested in ensuring clean water for the needy public.

Until the Age of Enlightenment, and even during this period, the water supply was still part of the private sector. During the eighteenth century, water was considered a private commodity. In London, water could not compete with beer and mulled wine, and it was explicitly called "the poor man's drink." Water was used mainly for drinking and cooking. During the Tudor period in England (sixteenth century), the use of mineral water was common for the purpose of fashionable drinking. This water was brought from bathhouses, such as Bath and Buxton, where bubbling mineral water flowed. This water was healthy by definition: pure spring water without any contamination from sewage or road water. Queen Elizabeth (1558–1603) kept a steady supply of such water, and the nobility of the kingdom drank it. This situation lasted about two hundred years. The situation in Germany, too, was similar. Most physicians in the eighteenth century would recommend which water sources were beneficial to health because of the iron, salts, and sulfur in the water.

Recognition of the universal need for clean water occurred to the policy makers in England and France only in the mid-nineteenth century. The method of transporting water in pipes and buckets did not address the needs of rapidly growing cities. Population growth in England in the nineteenth century was very high: In the first half of the century the population grew from 9 million to 18 million inhabitants. The urban population in Manchester grew from 75,000 to 303,000, and the population in Birmingham grew from 71,000 to 233,000. The water supply system did not keep pace, and the use of contaminated river water caused serious health problems. It was clear that water quality was deteriorating. Commissions of inquiry wrote reports that were shelved, but then catastrophe struck: the cholera epidemic of 1831–1832 killed 31,474 people in England and 25,378 in Ireland, and it was clear that the murky waters were at least a part of the disaster's cause. The disease caused national panic, and the overwhelming feeling was that a radical solution must be found.

Edwin Chadwick, a social activist, discovered with the aid of some doctors that cholera epidemics are not caused by spoiled food, stale air, or even poverty, but rather by poor sanitary conditions that harm water quality. His report[2] explained exactly how intestinal diseases are transmitted and how pandemics are created. Chadwick's argument was that improving water quality was essential for both health and economic reasons (to prevent loss of productivity), as well as for reasons of public morale, and cited a budgetary rationale that was original at the time. He argued that governmental support for the poor would be reduced if heads of families did not die at an early age.

When a cholera epidemic broke out again in 1848, improved sanitation was still a distant vision, but it was now clear what the solution was. The epidemic killed 60,293 civilians in England in less than a year, and again it was determined that impure water was the main cause. By that time, citizens had begun to take preventive measures, such as adding alcohol to water before drinking it or boiling it before using it for domestic use. Soft

---

2   Edwin Chadwick, *Report on the Sanitary Conditions of the Labouring Population of Great Britian*, 1842.

drinks in bottles began to be marketed. Schweppes sold more than a million bottles of soft drinks and carbonated water in 1851. Water suppliers from health springs (i.e., mineral water) worked overtime to meet the demand. Doctors recommended drinking hot drinks, such as tea and coffee, and their consumption also increased. Another phenomenon was the supply of water purification filters, which helped to remove particles but did not solve the problem of bacteria.

By the second half of the nineteenth century, the authorities had begun to solve the problem of supplying good drinking water. The issue became a municipal matter, and the solution involved large investments. Realization grew that the private market alone would not be able to finance the large projects required for this purpose. Market forces required public aid, due both to the requisite scope and the necessary uniformity of the solution. No less difficult was the need to improve the disposal of garbage and sewage. In London, this was carried out by an engineer named Joseph Bazalgette in the years 1859–1865. In Paris, the task was achieved by Baron Haussmann, who renovated the city under order of Napoleon III.

The medical research that was developed in Europe at the time helped to understand the issues of water purification. Due to the work of Louis Pasteur, who isolated the cholera bacteria in 1867, and Robert Koch's explanation of postulates in 1883, it became possible to solve problems of pollutants visible only through a microscope. Following the epidemics and intestinal diseases of the nineteenth century, Western Europe now knew what the problem was and what the solution was, and as they say, "the rest is history." Mortality from various intestinal diseases, from typhus to cholera, declined notably after 1880. Public works improved the quality of drinking water primarily by separating the sewage system from the water supply system. At the end of the nineteenth century, G. Sims Woodhead provided a method of purifying water through chlorination. Chlorination has been widely used since the 1920s.

4. What's Happening Today?

In today's Western world, tap water and bottled water seem natural. There is indeed a charge for water but there is no problem of quantity, and our basic need is filled by turning on the tap. In contrast, in the Third World, the supply of pure or any kind of water is not taken for granted. More than half the population in Africa lives more than a quarter of an hour's walk from a water source, from which water can be taken home in buckets or jerry cans. In Senegal, women spend about 17 hours a week carrying water in containers for domestic use. In Mozambique, that number is 15.3 hours per week on average. There, too, when the local well or the public tap provides brackish water, the poorer population is forced to pay private water suppliers, who bring drinking water in trucks to the population centers.

So what can be done? According to the United Nations,[3] the intention is to bring good quality water to half of the needy population, but the implementation is not simple: Since 1980, the United Nations has declared every decade a global effort to supply drinking water and sanitation (The International Drinking Water Supply and Sanitation Decade), yet the situation has not improved significantly. The current assessment is that a significant

---

3   www.un.org/millenniumgoals

improvement in the water and sewage infrastructure in developing countries will require $100 billion by 2035. Poor countries cannot raise such an amount, and international agencies will find it difficult. This is the backdrop for the debate over privatization of the water sector. Those who favor privatization believe that it will raise resources for building the proper infrastructure and will create access to pure water for large communities in the developing world. The arguments for or against the privatization of the water sector are similar to claims for or against the privatization of other public services, which are usually made on the grounds that the governments are unable to provide these services by themselves. Similar arguments are being held over toll roads and schools. Those who support privatization argue that private management is more effective because it is cut off from local politicians. Opponents emphasize the citizens' right to receive free services from the state, without being obligated to pay the cost of setting up the infrastructure.

And what is the situation in the Middle East? Israel itself does not suffer from water shortages. The combination of recycled water, proper pricing, and seawater desalination has resulted in a continuous supply and prevention of shortages. This is not the situation in Israel's immediate vicinity. Jordan, for example, must cope with a continuous shortage of water and imports water from Israel. In Amman, the capital of Jordan, water leaks from the municipal pipeline and water shutoffs are normal. In Lebanon, for the time being, there is no shortage of water. In contrast, in Egypt, water sources are shrinking in relation to population growth. Already today there are about ten million Egyptian citizens suffering from a shortage of drinking water. Syria had an ongoing water crisis even before the outbreak of the civil war in 2011. One million farmers had to move to the cities to seek a livelihood when the amount of water used for agriculture plummeted. The main reason for this is the dams built by the Turkish government on the Euphrates River, which reduced the flow of water to Syria and Iraq.

Households in Israel enjoy a regular water supply, and Israeli farmers use water according to their needs, including purified water and partial saltwater suitable for irrigation. The amount of precipitation in Israel is about 1.2 billion cubic meters per year, and the national water consumption is almost double that. The answer to this situation is desalination. A visitor to the Palmachim desalination plant can see how a glass of saltwater from the Mediterranean Sea turns into a glass of drinking water within twenty minutes. The process requires the use of electricity (taken only in hours of reduced load) and a skilled work force, but the desalinated water in this facility provides 7 percent of the country's needs. In total, desalinated water constitutes one-third of Israel's water consumption, and the other two-thirds is natural water.

A lack of readiness to recognize that water is a product in short supply has its price. Economists argue that the absence of appropriate pricing for water causes excessive consumption. The prevailing perception today is that the private market is superior to the government market in appropriate pricing and the allocation of shortage products. For this reason, international organizations grant loans for drinking water projects only if they are run by private companies that set a suitable price. However, it is still accepted that a municipal water supply holds a "natural monopoly" that benefits from economies of scale, thus creating entry barriers for private competitors. Many still object to privatization, and they demand adherence to the vision of the prophets. The difficulty with that is that the prophets assumed that an individual goes to the water source and not that the water is transported to the individual at a price that does not cover the cost.

An interesting phenomenon in recent years is the extent of drinking bottled water. This phenomenon is characteristic of developed countries, although in these countries tap water is usually safe from a health standpoint. Italians drink an average of 190 liters of mineral water per person per year. And the French, the Belgians, the Dutch, and the Germans are not far behind the Italians. The global bottled water industry sells about $60 billion worth of water a year (data from 2009), and consumption is growing from year to year. Cafes and restaurants serve cold water in glass bottles designed by top fashion designers. Football players and top models walk around with bottles of water in their hands or in a fashionable bag. It was not so at the beginning of the twenty-first century, but it is happening now. Mineral water from Italy and France is sold all over the world as a luxury drink.

Bottled water consumption is based on the belief that this water is safer and healthier than tap water, which is offered almost free everywhere and is also available and prominent in public parks and entertainment venues. However, as a rule, tap water in developed countries is as safe as bottled water. Moreover, some of the water sold in the designer bottles is actually ordinary tap water. About 40 percent of the bottled water in the United States is ordinary tap water that has simply been filtered, and sometimes minerals are added. Regardless of the true source of the water, the bottles feature pictures of snowy mountains, springs, and waterfalls.

There is no concrete evidence that the water in bottles is safer and healthier than conventional urban tap water, yet a majority of the public still prefers it. It is possible to estimate the degree of preference when we recall that bottled water is four hundred times more expensive than simple tap water. In contrast, in the less developed countries, more than one billion citizens have no access to pure water. The World Health Organization reports that 80 percent of the world's diseases originate from contaminated water. Diseases such as diarrhea, tapeworms, trachoma, and more are caused by polluted drinking water, causing the deaths of nearly two million people a year (90 percent of them children). From my personal experience in water purification, I can testify that underdeveloped countries have no means of establishing national water systems or water purification regions. The UN Water Quality Improvement Program estimates that the spending on this will be $9 billion a year, and as yet no budget has been found.

5. And What about the Future?

Future water supply depends on three factors. First, the growing number of inhabitants on the planet. Second, climate changes that may affect the quantity and geographical distribution of water. Third, the pricing of water that can have an impact on its proper utilization and prevent shortages.

As the population grows, so does the use of water, and there are few places where water is priced at the marginal cost of producing it. Usually the price of water is intentionally low. Politicians are afraid to charge a high or full price for water, and as a result, consumers have no incentive to save water, and investors have no incentive to build infrastructures that will allow water to be delivered to places where it is needed. Examples abound. In South

Africa, a certain amount of free water is distributed to all households. In Sri Lanka, consumers pay 4 cents per cubic meter, while the covering cost is close to 160 cents. These are just examples of the normal standard of an inappropriate price, which causes a large deficit in the financing of the world's water infrastructure.

In some countries, water can be pumped from underground aquifers for agricultural purposes almost without restriction. Such action may seem reasonable, but the water drawn from these reservoirs is also used to grow crops in "dry" areas unsuitable for water-intensive crops, which is clearly unsustainable. Dr. Moshe Frumer, an expert on water purification, used to say that people do not consume much water for personal use, and that five liters per day is sufficient for a person to drink, cook, and wash. This is true, but population growth requires an increase in the food supply, and that also requires water. Let me present a few examples for thought: In order to grow one kilogram of wheat, 1,200 liters of water are needed during the growing season. Raising one cow that will provide meat will require ten times more water than that. Today, the world's population is 7.5 billion, and to feed it, agriculture consumes 70 percent of the world's sweet water.

Water is needed not only for the production of food and household use. It is also important for economic growth. Electricity generation, for example, requires a great deal of water. Nuclear energy production also requires an immense amount of water to cool the nuclear reactor. With the development of poor countries, the demand for electricity in these countries will rise by 300 percent by the middle of the twenty-first century. Most industries that consume large amounts of water—such as textiles, wood, and chemistry—are found in countries that are particularly prone to water shortages (China, India, and Australia). Worse still, the burgeoning industry can damage our water supply by polluting the sources.

Climate changes are expected to make the situation worse. Experts believe global warming will accelerate the cycle of evaporation, condensation, and precipitation. Wet areas will become wetter, and dry areas will dry out completely. In addition, the rate of fluid loss in the soil and in most plant species will accelerate, and late or sparse rains will change the rate of refilling water reservoirs and aquifers. Another problem is dwindling snowfall in a warming world. Many countries are dependent on snow that melts in the mountains and flows into the plains towards the summer. Variable climate patterns may cause crops to fail where they have been successfully grown in the past. In Africa, crops are expected to shrink by 20 percent if the average temperature rises by a mere two degrees Celsius. The dryness and heat will no longer allow legumes to be grown in East Africa (Kenya, Uganda, and Tanzania).

Since agriculture often uses water, it is also an important target to save water. Proper planting and hybrid seeds that require less watering can help conserve water. Our well-known irrigation drips transfer water directly to plant roots, thereby reducing the use of water by 40–70 percent as opposed to other irrigation methods. Water for agriculture can also be supplied by recycling wastewater. Israel recycles nearly 80 percent of its sewage (while Spain, for example, recycles only 20 percent). The potential savings in the world through recycling is very large. Singapore, for example, recycles sewage and transforms it into drinking water, but this is a special case.

The water shortage is also due to the lack of investment in infrastructure. Leaking pipes in many Middle Eastern cities cause a loss of some 60 percent of the drinking water. London also loses 30 percent of its drinking water due to leaky pipes. Poorer countries, where millions of people live in poor neighborhoods without proper sanitation, need not only pipes, but also reservoirs and purification plants. The establishment of these depends on our willingness to invest. Desalination plants, such as those in Saudi Arabia and Israel, turn seawater into drinking water, but the process is expensive because of the quantities of electricity needed to do so. Therefore, water desalination for agricultural purposes is still not on the agenda.

Chapter Two

WINE THAT GLADDENS HUMAN HEARTS

1. Ancient History

Wine has served humanity as an important drink since prehistoric times. Archaeological evidence from the Neolithic period shows that nearly four thousand years ago, wine was used in the Zagros Mountains (Iran and Armenia). Jewish tradition also mentions wine[1] in this region, albeit in a later period. Noah, son of Lamech, survived the flood, and when the water receded, it was said: "Noah, a man of the soil, planted a vineyard. And he drank of the wine, and became drunk, and was uncovered in his tent" (Genesis 9:20–21). This was not far from the mountain range of Zagros, near Mount Ararat on which the ark landed when the flood ended.

Wine is made from fermented grape juice or crushed grapes. Natural yeast, found on grape skins, turns the sugar in the grapes into alcohol. Originally, any attempt to preserve grapes or grape juice (in a clay jar, for example) ended in the production of wine. Archaeological evidence of the existence of wine was based on an examination of the interiors of pottery vessels that were found stained reddish from the wine that was stored in them. From its birthplace in the region of Ararat, wine spread over the years to

---

1   The title of the present chapter is a quote from Psalm 104:15.

the entire Middle East. At first, wine was intended for kings and ministers, then for nobility, and over time it became a popular drink for all classes of the population.

The practice of growing grapes for making wine also arrived in Greece. The Greeks planted vineyards alongside olive trees and fig trees, and wine there was also a beverage of the political elites. In Assyria, in the Fertile Crescent, wine was no longer a symbol of wealth and political power, and the wine trade began. At first, trade was local and later became international. Cuneiform tablets, in the Assyrian city of Nimrud, note that wine was also given to the king's servants. The wine was distributed, in quantities similar to today's liter, in clay jars. Each jar was intended to provide drinks for ten simple laborers or for six professional workers, who received larger portions.

Trade increased when wine became a commodity for the general public. The Greek historian Herodotus described boats laden with wine sailing on the Euphrates and Tigris to the south. It seems that at the time (in the fifth century BCE), wine was a relatively cheap commodity. The Book of Daniel mentions the wine that was drunk in Babylon, and Nehemiah writes explicitly: "And I carried the wine and gave it to the king" (Nehemiah 2:1). There are several references to wine in the Bible, including in the Book of Genesis: "And Melchizedek king of Salem brought forth bread and wine" (Genesis 14:18). The results of excessive drinking (i.e., drunkenness) are mentioned in the case of Noah and in the case of Lot, whose daughters say: "Come, let us make our father drink wine..." (Genesis 19:32). In other books, too, wine is mentioned, as in those of the prophets Isaiah, Jeremiah, Zachariah, and Hosea. Wine also features in the Book of Esther: "when the heart of the king was merry with wine..." (Esther 1:10), and is mentioned in the Song of Songs as a measure of pleasure: "How much better is your love than wine..." (Song of Songs 4:10).

2. What Happened in Ancient Greece?

What can be said in this context about Greece in the sixth and fifth centuries BCE, during the golden age? Greece bequeathed to the Western world the foundations of philosophy, science, law, and democracy. But ancient Greece was not a monolithic country. It had many "city-states" that fought each other, made occasional alliances, and cooperated against common enemies.

The Greek aristocracy held meetings for philosophical discussions, with consumption of wine, that were called *symposiums*. During these events they would speak words of wisdom, sing, and make speeches, and their intellectual pursuits were accompanied by the drinking of wine. The historian Thucydides noted, in the fifth century BCE, that the people of the Mediterranean began to emerge from barbarism when they learned to cultivate olives and vines. The Greeks did this before others, and Greek playwright Euripides writes in his play *Bacchae* that both rich and poor Greeks enjoyed the pleasures of wine, which also served as a cure for pain.

From the seventh century BCE, the Greeks cultivated vineyards throughout the Hellenic Peninsula. The historian and poet Hesiod describes, in his poem *Works and Days*, how to prune vine branches, when to harvest grapes, and how to make wine from them. The Greeks improved the extraction of the grape juice and contributed to the cultivation of vines in straight, stacked lines (instead of scattered) on high stakes, in order to obtain a high yield from a given unit area. The cultivation of grape vines was more profitable to farmers in classical Greece than the cultivation of wheat. Therefore, Greece exported wine to other countries and imported wheat. Wine grapes were also grown on the islands of Lesvos, Tilos, and Chios, off the western coast of Turkey. Dionysus, the Greek god of nature and fertility, is also identified as the god of the grape harvest and wine.

As wine became more of a commodity, the poorer city dwellers also drank it, and even slaves drank wine. High quality wine was of course consumed by the aristocracy, and poorer quality wine was consumed by the common people. Alongside the wine quality distinction, ancient Greece also began to differentiate between regions where the grapes were grown to produce wine. The philosopher and poet Archestratus, who lived in Sicily in the fourth century BCE, notes in his tome *Gastronomy* (which was mainly a cookbook) that the best wine was produced on the island of Lesvos. The ancient Greeks also paid attention to vintage, and older wine became desirable. The Greeks drank sweet wine as well, and Homer's *Odyssey* notes that Odysseus kept sweet wine for himself.

3. A Little More about the Symposium

An important social event in ancient Greece, as already mentioned, was the *symposium* (banquet). A special room, called the *andrōn*, was usually assigned to the symposium, and its walls were decorated with various paintings. Sometimes it was the only room in a house that had a stone floor. The event was attended by between twelve and twenty guests, men only, who reclined on couches. Women were not included among the participants but were allowed to wait on those in the symposium by serving food, dancing, or playing instruments.

The symposium opened with a meal. The dishes were then cleared from the table, wreaths of flowers were distributed to each participant, and the wine was poured into a large serving jar (*krater*), in which the wine was diluted with varying degrees of water. A mixture in which the quantity of wine equaled the amount of water was considered strong wine, and there were usually weaker mixtures (i.e., more water and less wine)—for example, at a ratio of two-, three-, or four-to-one. The symposium continued as the guests drank the wine. The diluted wine was a safer drink than water, for the alcohol killed the bacteria in the water and served as a healing remedy. Water-diluted wine was also considered suitable for preventing intoxication.

The clay pitchers the guests drank from at the symposium were decorated with paintings related to drinking wine. At first these consisted of paintings solely in black, later also in fine red. The wealthy drank from silver goblets. During the drinking, there were exchanges between the participants, and sometimes also public singing and recitations. The philosopher Plato wrote about the symposium in a positive manner, recalling, among other observations, Socrates's ability to remain alert even after drinking a large quantity of wine. The philosopher Xenophon wrote, in the middle of the fourth century BCE, that arguing while drinking wine sharpens thought. He believed that wine reduces passion and anger, thus contributing to a calm discussion during a symposium.

Greece, in ancient times, exported wine to every land bordering the Mediterranean: from southern France to Egypt, from Algeria to the Crimean Peninsula. Pottery jugs called amphorae have been found in excavations in these lands. The jugs were used to transport wine in carts and ships, usually only in one direction. After drinking the wine, people would discard the jugs. In tombs discovered in southern France (dated to the fourth century BCE), nobles were found buried alongside wine-serving vessels (pitchers and cups).

4. Conceptual Exercise: Wine in Rome

In the second century BCE, after the victory over Carthage, Rome became the leading force in the Mediterranean basin. The Romans adopted large parts of Greek culture, and there were distinguished Romans who claimed, at the time, with dry humor, that military victory was a cultural failure. The Greek gods were adopted by the Romans but given different names. The culture of imbibing wine was preserved as in Greece, and the "boot" of Italy became a wine-producing region. Vines were planted in Italy, and the wine flowed in large quantities. The historian Pliny the Elder wrote, in 70 CE, that two-thirds of all wine in the Mediterranean was made from grapes grown in Italy.

The success of viniculture in Italy led to the conversion of land from production of wheat to production of wine grapes, and it became necessary to import wheat from North Africa. Thus a parallel trade developed—the Romans imported wheat and exported wine to Mediterranean countries. The wine was exported on ships carrying up to three thousand amphorae made of clay, and other light loads of oil and nuts. Many cracked amphorae have been found in shipwrecks from this period. The amphorae were transported in one direction and were discarded after the wine was drunk. Amphora remains have been found in garbage dumps in Marseilles, Athens, and Alexandria. Later, during the period of the empire, the Romans used wooden barrels for storing and transporting wine, and these barrels could be reused.

Fine wine also found its way to Rome. The jars, and later the wooden barrels as well, were transported on small boats that sailed up the Tiber from Ostia harbor to the center of the city. There, the wine was stored in basements and distributed via shops and market stalls. The nobility of Rome sent their slaves to buy the wine from local merchants. The Romans learned to value the quality of the wine, and good wines were sold at a great price. Fine "Falernian" wine was made from vines that grew on the slopes of Mount Falernus, south of Naples. This wine was savored by Julius Caesar and other emperors, and the poets praised it in their poems.

While the rich in Rome enjoyed fine wine, the lower classes drank simpler wine. At festive events called *convivia*, they distinguished between the various classes by serving wine suited to the status of each guest. As mentioned, there was no class discrimination in the Greek symposium, and all the participants drank the same wine.

Like the Greeks, the Romans drank wine mixed with water, but in Rome each guest drank wine according to his will. The seating arrangement at the convivium was not as egalitarian as in the symposium, and some seats were considered better than others. The convivium therefore reflected the accepted class hierarchy. The Roman system established the relationship between client and patron. The plebian client supported the patrician patron, and the patron paid him occasionally. The client also accompanied the patron and supported him in his political endeavors. Wine consumption reflected this reality. The historian Pliny the Younger noted three types of wine that were graded according to their quality: superior wine for patrons, average wine for clients who were citizens of Rome, and inferior wine for liberated slaves.

Average wines would occasionally have cherry juice or honey added to them to improve the taste. It was also common to add herbs to average wines to improve their flavor. This was especially common in the Roman army. The Roman soldier who offered to wipe Jesus's face during the Crucifixion used a cloth soaked in wine. Even the slaves in Rome drank wine, but it was a simple and cheap wine (called *lora*) of very poor quality.

5. Wine and Medicine

Claudius Galenus (129–c. 200 CE) was considered to be the greatest physician of the ancient world. He studied medicine in his hometown of Pergamon in Asia Minor, and later in Egypt. As a young man, he worked as a physician at the Pergamon Gladiator School, where he specialized in surgery and began to write treatises on medicine, especially sports medicine and general hygiene. In 162 he moved to Rome and stayed there for several years. He gave lectures on medicine and demonstrated his theories by experimenting with animals. In 166 he left Rome and returned to Pergamon. In 169, Emperor Marcus Aurelius invited him to return to Rome as the imperial court physician. Thanks to his scientific activity, he was considered an excellent doctor. Galenus wrote many books, and his influence on the medical profession lasted until the fifteenth century.

Like his predecessors in the ancient world, Galenus believed that sickness stemmed mainly from an imbalance between the four humors: blood, white bile (phlegm), yellow bile, and black bile (from the liver). It was possible, in his opinion, to restore the balance between these fluids by bloodletting, eating appropriate food, drinking wine, and other methods. We will not go into Galenus's theory in depth but note that he had a special interest in wine. When, for example, he treated the wounds of the Pergamon gladiators, he used wine as a disinfectant, and he believed that wine had additional healing properties.

Galenus used wine as a medicine for Emperor Marcus Aurelius to reduce yellow bile. He also used wine as a medicine for chills and colds. In the emperor's wine cellars, he sought the best wine for healing and tasted different types of Falernian wine. He required twenty tastings until he found the best wine, which he recommended to the emperor as a medicine for colds and protection against other diseases. He also concocted a mixture to protect the emperor from poisoning. It had many ingredients, but its base was wine.

In the centuries after the fall of the Roman Empire, wine-drinking culture waned, and international trade in wine declined greatly. On the Christian side of the Mediterranean, however, wine played a part in rituals and prayers, and a little was consumed every weekend, but the quantity declined. During this time, the rise of Islam impacted on wine drinking. Islam forbade the drinking of wine, and the ban led to a sharp reduction in grape growing in the Middle East and in North Africa.

6. Wine After the Decline of Rome

In the Middle Ages, wine continued to be a favorite beverage in southern Europe, where the weather was suitable for growing grapes. From there the wine was sent out in barrels, albeit not in large quantities, to the countries of northern Europe. Much of the wine production during this period was in the hands of Catholic orders, such as the Carthusians and the Templars. Especially prominent was the Benedictine Order, which cultivated large tracts of vineyards in Champagne, Burgundy, and Bordeaux. Dom Pérignon, who perfected the production of Champagne, was a Benedictine monk. In Germany, too, there was active wine production, with white Riesling wines playing a leading role. Portugal was also a region of wine growing at this time.

The wine trade was influenced by politics. During the reign of Henry II in England, the English were great importers of wine from Bordeaux. However, at the end of the Hundred Years' War (1453), imports from France stopped. In the period between 1700 and 1860, the United Kingdom levied a particularly high tariff on wines imported from France. In contrast, the British imported large quantities of port wine from Portugal.

After America was discovered, grapevines were planted in several countries on this continent. Hernán Cortés, governor of Mexico, ordered the planting of vineyards in Mexico in 1525. Their success forced the king of Spain, in 1595, to order a ban on planting grapevines in Mexico so that local wine production in Spain would not be harmed. In spite of this, the wine industry continued in Catholic monasteries. In 1769, the Franciscan priest Junípero Serra planted the first vineyards in California (then under Spanish rule), in the San Diego area. Later, Masonic monasteries were also built in northern California, and vineyards of wine grapes were planted around each one. The process continued after California passed into the hands of the United States. Vineyards were also planted in northern California, and small wineries engaged in production and storage. Over time, California became an international wine producer.

7. Wine and the Scientific Revolution

For hundreds of years, wine was produced in many countries in ignorance of the biology of the grapevine and the chemistry of wine. Scientific knowledge entered public consciousness when Louis Pasteur published his research on wine in 1857, proving that wine was produced by a type of bacteria—yeast that is found in nature. His discovery led to an understanding of the role and function of yeast, and subsequently to improved hygiene and a reduction in the spoiling of wine stored in barrels.

In 1863, several species of American vines were brought to botanical gardens in England. These seedlings carried aphids originating in the Mississippi Valley, and the pest spread across Europe, mainly in France. The aphid was a familiar insect in the United States, and the vines there were immune to it. No one imagined what devastation the aphid could cause in Europe. In 1865 the aphid began to spread across the vineyards of Provence. The aphid, called phylloxera (*Phylloxera vastatrix*), eats the roots of the vine and causes them to rot, destroying the entire plant. For twenty years vine-growers tried to fight phylloxera by flooding and spraying the soil with carbon dioxide, a costly and inefficient process. The vineyards of Europe were dying, and wine was becoming scarce. Fortunately, a Texas botanist named Thomas Munson understood that if the vines in America had a natural immunity to phylloxera, the European species could be grafted onto the roots of American vines. His suggestion was accepted, and the problem was solved.

Following the blight and its remedy by grafting, local vines in France flourished once again, but some of the species that had been popular before the blight were lost forever. Another effect stemmed from the shortage itself: when wine was less available, the custom of diluting wine with water grew. For this reason, a mandatory wine standard, entitled *appellation d'origine contrôlée*, was established in France, in order to ensure that the wine was not diluted and met an agreed standard. Another phenomenon was the flourishing of the Northern California wine industry. The quality of California wines was comparable to European quality in 1900, and other wines produced in the United States became market leaders. In the early twentieth century, barrels of American wine were exported to, among other locations, South America and Australia.

8. Wine and Politics in the United States

The main damage to the wine production industry in the United States did not come from the aphid or any other pest but was entirely man-made. In the nineteenth century, excessive consumption of alcohol leading to drunkenness was considered a harmful phenomenon in the United States, and governments fought it by banning the drinking of alcohol. The first law prohibiting the sale of alcoholic beverages (including wine) on Sundays was enacted in Indiana in 1816 and is valid to this day. Over the next twenty years, similar laws were enacted in Georgia, Michigan, and other states. By 1851, New York and Ohio had also joined what were then called the "dry states." By 1855, thirteen states (out of the thirty-one that composed the United States) limited the sale of alcohol in their jurisdictions.

In 1880, the state of Kansas passed a law forbidding the sale of alcoholic beverages within its borders, and several other states (Mississippi, North Carolina, Tennessee, and Virginia) followed suit. Wine was included in the ban, but beer was allowed, so wine sales in restaurants and bars decreased and beer sales increased. Although it was permissible to manufacture and export wine, the ban on consumption within the country greatly reduced demand. Many wineries closed, and planting of vines halted. The principle of dryness was bolstered by religious activists who lobbied to remove the words *wine* and *alcohol* from school textbooks. The sale of medicinal wines was also banned in pharmacies.

In December 1917, the United States Congress passed the Eighteenth Amendment to the Constitution, which made the production and sale of alcohol illegal in a sweeping prohibition under criminal law. By February 1919, the amendment had been approved by forty-five states (New Jersey, Connecticut, and Rhode Island did not have the necessary majority for approval). The law required for the enforcement of the National Prohibition Act was passed later the same year, and from January 1920 it was forbidden to manufacture, sell, or consume alcohol in public throughout the United States. Private consumption was not prohibited by federal law, but in practice it was difficult to purchase such drinks. The results of the "dry law" are known: the smuggling of alcoholic beverages imported from Canada or Mexico increased, and the local police in each state had to bear an excessive workload. During this period, the FBI was also founded in order, among other reasons, to reduce crime stemming from the "dry law." In the 1920s, more policemen were killed in the United States than in any other decade of the twentieth century.

As a consequence of liquor smuggling and the increase in crime, it became clear that Prohibition was not a good law, or at least could not be successfully enforced, and in December 1933 the law was repealed. Although a number of states maintained the prohibition of alcohol consumption in their jurisdictions (Kansas, Oklahoma, and Mississippi, for example), in most of the United States it was again possible to produce and buy alcohol. But the wine industry was devastated, and the liquor industry was also in bad shape. The import gates opened for wine, and the public could buy again fine, expensive European wines. Local manufacturers quickly began to produce simple, inferior wines made from poor-quality vines, which led the public to avoid local wine consumption.

On the other hand, fortified wines that had an alcohol content of 20 percent registered success. The American whiskey industry also returned to normal production within a short time.

Prior to 1920 there were 2,500 wineries in the United States. In 1933, when the constitutional prohibition on the sale of wine was repealed, only 100 wineries remained. By 1960, the number of wineries had increased to 271. It took fifty years (up to the mid-1980s) before the industry recovered, and it was only in the late 1970s that table wine returned to the position it had held in the US, comprising 75 percent of alcohol consumption (excluding beer). At the beginning of the twenty-first century, 4,383 wineries were registered in the United States, and the wines of the Napa Valley in California (mainly Chardonnay and Cabernet Sauvignon) compete today with the best in the world.

9. Kosher Wine

Archaeological findings show that there was a great deal of wine production in ancient Israel. This is no surprise, given that every Sabbath, Jews must make a blessing over wine during the Kiddush. Every Jewish child knows the blessing "Blessed are You, O Lord our God, King of the Universe, Creator of the fruit of the vine." At the Passover Seder, Jews are commanded to drink four cups of wine, and on Purim a Jew must drink wine "until he knows not between cursed Haman and blessed Mordechai."

The Jews therefore have a long history of drinking wine, but of course we are speaking of kosher wine. In order for wine to be kosher, it must be made by Sabbath-observant Jews involved in all stages of its production. Kosher for Passover wine is wine made in an environment where there is no leavening of any kind. Another concept that should be mentioned in this context is *mevushal* wine (cooked or boiled). Mevushal wine is wine that is heated to a temperature of seventy-five degrees Celsius—in other words, without bubbling or boiling. The heating is akin to pasteurization.

In the golden age of Spain, Jewish courtiers and the wealthy of the community would invite a large crowd to participate in family events, such as circumcisions, bar mitzvahs, and weddings, or events marking commercial achievements. At these parties, the guests were offered wine mixed with water, as was customary in Greece and Rome during the classical period. How diluted was the wine? At times, the wine was diluted with up to 80 percent water, and its effect was barely felt.

10. Nice to Know

After World War II, and especially in the 1950s and 1960s, there was a surplus supply of wine in the United States. The wine industry was then compelled to educate the general public about wine identification. This was an "educational" program that succeeded. The training is summarized below.

When you enter a wine shop or wine department of a supermarket, it is easy to identify wines by **color**. There is white wine, red wine, and rosé wine. All wines are made from grapes, of course. The color of the wine depends on the grapes used in its production and the presence or absence of the grape skins. White wine is made from grapes that have been crushed and the juice extracted, with the skins removed from the pulp, while red wine is made from grape pulp that also includes the skins. Another important difference is the duration of maturation. White wine can be drunk immediately after fermenting properly and does not need to be stored in barrels. But red wine improves when it is stored in oak barrels for a year or two. Rosé wines are usually made from special varieties of grapes whose pulp is pinkish (flushed) from the start.

So, the first way to identify wine is by color. A second way is by the degree of **fermentation** in the final product. There are standard table wines in the three colors described, and there are sparkling wines. The most well-known white wine is sparkling French Champagne, usually made from Chardonnay or Pinot Noir grapes. There are also good sparkling wines from Italy, such as Prosecco, and Cava from Spain, among others. Without going into the production process again, it is easy to identify a sparkling wine made in the French method, because when poured into a glass, bubbles rise from the bottom to the rim of the glass. This indicates that the wine has not been artificially carbonated. Champagne-style wines are served chilled, and during a meal the bottle sits in a metal container filled with ice, known as a champagne bucket.

An additional test for identifying wines is the level of **sweetness**. White wines are classified according to sweetness: "dry," "semidry," and "sweet." (Sometimes there is also "very sweet" white wine.) The higher the sugar level, the less dry the wine. Dry or semidry wine is usually drunk with a meal, and sweet wine is used for dessert. White wines are usually made from Emerald Riesling, Muscat, Chenin Blanc, or Sémillon grapes. Red wines are usually made from Cabernet Sauvignon (the most common) grapes, Merlot, Shiraz, Barbera, Chianti, or Sirah. Cabernet Sauvignon produces a deep wine with a purple color. Merlot produces red wine that is fruitier and purpler. Shiraz is a stronger wine with a dominant flavor that is felt at the first sip.

A stroll around wine shelves reveals that most wines are produced in only a few countries. France is considered the leader in the global wine market, closely followed by Spain and Italy, each with regions of vineyards that produce soft wines and harder wines with strong flavor. Germany specializes in white wines, and Portugal specializes in rosé wines that taste slightly sour. Outside Europe, the United States, Australia, and Chile should be mentioned. There are other countries that produce good wine, such as Greece and Israel, but they are less active on the international market.

When it comes to producing wine from grapes, one should remember that it is an organic product that requires appropriate climatic conditions to supply large quantities of good quality. This is an agricultural sector whose output varies according to the conditions. There are dry years, years of hot winds, and years of frostbite that harm crops. Producers, therefore, mark on each bottle the "year of birth," or vintage of the grapes from which the wine was made. There are "good" years when good wine is produced, and there are "bad years" when less good wine is produced. Connoisseurs among us can tell the difference.

11. What Goes with What? A Leisurely Ceremony

What goes with what? Wine is mainly consumed at meals, and the basic question is how to match a wine to a particular food. The traditional recommendation is to link the color of the wine to the color of the meat. Red wines are suitable for red meat, and light wines are suitable for light foods, such as fish and chicken. Some add the recommendation to drink good but simple wine. A separate problem involves matching wines and desserts. In Europe, it is customary to make sure that the wine is sweeter than the dessert. Desserts may include cakes, fruit salads, puddings, jellies, ice cream, sorbet, and more. The above rule is often broken, and this is acceptable. Pink rosé wines are also considered suitable for every dish.

When eating in a restaurant, one is given a wine menu, which usually includes a "house wine" that can be ordered by bottle, carafe (glass flask), or glass. This wine option is sometimes off-menu, so care should be taken when choosing. The house wine is also served in glasses and can be tasted before ordering a carafe. There are wines marketed in bottles of 375 milliliters, which contain three glasses, while a regular bottle of 750 millili-ters contains six glasses. The choice of half a bottle is also suitable for those who want to start with white wine and continue with red for the main course. Incidentally, one should not to be embar-rassed to ask the price of each bottle, if this is not explicitly stated on the wine menu.

After the desired wine is selected from the wine menu, the ceremony continues. The waiter arrives and asks who is the "official taster" for the table. He then shows the taster the bottle to verify that the correct wine has been brought. It is particu-larly important to check the vintage, since a wine is sometimes served not from the vintage that was ordered. If the restaurant is meticulous, the waiter opens the bottle and gives the cork to the taster. This is to demonstrate that the cork did not crumble, does not have a moldy smell, and, in particular, is wet on the inner side (indicating that the wine was stored lying down). After presenting the cork, the waiter pours a little wine into a glass. The taster is supposed to look at the wine to make sure it is not cloudy and then taste it. Jeff Rosenblum, an expert on California wines, says that the goal of the tasting is not to check whether a wine tastes good, but only to make sure that it is not spoiled and has been served at the right temperature. In very unusual cases when the wine has a bad smell or is cloudy, one can ask for another bottle to be opened.

We should mention that we also eat at home and buy our wines in shops. In this case it is important to pay attention to several details. First, it is important to identify the name of the winery and the series to which the wine belongs. Wineries have popular series, and series that are considered prestigious, which are usually called "reserve." Second, it is advisable to read the name of the grape variety from which the wine was made. It can be a single variety ("varietal") containing at least 85 percent of one grape, or of several grapes. Third, it is customary to take note of the region where the grapes were grown. Fourth, one should pay attention to the description of the color of the wine, its level of sweetness (is it dry?), and the alcohol content in the wine. Finally, vintage can be important.

The purchased wine should be stored horizontally in a place that is not close to a heat source, such as a radiator or baking oven. If you drink large quantities of wine, you should consider a special refrigerator. White wine is usually served cold, at eight–twelve degrees Celsius, after several hours of cooling in the refrigerator. Sparkling wine should be served colder, at four–six degrees, and kept on ice during the meal. Red wine is usually served at room temperature of sixteen–twenty-two degrees Celsius.

12. Wine in the Islamic World and Local Varieties

Drunkenness from drinking alcohol is considered a serious crime in the Muslim world. A Muslim who drinks wine is subject to punishments that vary from one country to another. A non-Muslim who lives in a Muslim country may drink alcohol but is required to obtain a license to do so. Muslim countries also impose high taxes on the import of intoxicating beverages, including wine. Interpretation of the laws of the Quran differs from country to country. Some countries are more liberal and some less. In some cases it is permissible to drink wine privately, as long as drunkenness is avoided. In other words, what is forbidden by this prohibition is drunkenness.

In Muslim countries, for example, in the Middle East and North Africa, people have abstained from drinking wine for the past fifteen hundred years, but they continue to eat grapes that were used in the distant past to produce wine. These grapes are used today to produce local wine that is different in flavor and appearance from international wines, such as Cabernet, Merlot, Chardonnay, and Sirah. In Israel, for example, there is a local wine called Bittuni wine. It is made from a grape variety that survived because it was delicious to eat and is now being used again to make wine. This wine is different from conventional varieties; its color is light, its alcohol content is low, and it is low in tannins. Local wines are not only found in Israel. Many countries grow varieties of local grapes for making wine that is different from the norm. Commercially, varieties specific to particular regions (such as Chianti in Tuscany, Italy) also sell well in other countries.

13. The Wine Production Process

The grape harvest is usually done in the early morning hours, which are cooler. The grapes are transferred to the winery, where they are crushed and de-stemmed (cluster stems removed) by the appropriate machines. The juice, called *must*, is fermented, turning the sugar in the grape into alcohol. Fermentation is done in stainless steel vats. For white wine, the must is separated from the grape skins immediately after crushing. For red wine, the grapes are fermented with the skins and only discarded after fermentation. Color, taste, and tannin are determined by the grape skins. Tannin is also found in oak wood, from which the aging barrels are produced. After aging, the wine is bottled and each bottle is closed with a cork to prevent excessive air from entering the bottle. The cork works well when wet, so bottles of wine should be stored in a horizontal position.

Wine is a delicious, nutritious, and intoxicating beverage, produced by fermenting alcohol from plant products containing sugar. Wine produced from grapes is the best known. Grape wine is an aqueous solution of organic and mineral substances. A liter of wine comprises an average of about 860 grams of water, 12 percent alcohol, and various acids. As noted, after the harvest, the grapes are crushed to extract the juice, or must. In the past this was done by treading on the grapes. Today it is done by a mechanical press that scoops grapes from the cluster and crushes them into juice. Then the juice is poured into vats in which it is fermented with yeast. During fermentation there is temperature and specific density control.

In the finished wine there is sometimes another slow fermentation of sugar residue. After about ten days, the liquid is transferred to other containers in order to separate it from the yeast that has sunk into it, and a month later the wine is filtered and transferred to barrels or other containers. After three to six months, a taste test is conducted for each container. Professional tasters inspect the wine for appearance, aroma, and flavor. The inspection also examines clarity and color. Sniffing a wine determines whether the smell is free of foreign odors and whether it has a special odor (such as Muscat). The tasting also determines the level of acidity (weak, pleasant, or excessive), bitterness, sweetness, and more. In the next stage, the wine is stored in wooden barrels (usually) and then siphoned into bottles.

14. Wine and Holy Ritual

The Gospels of the New Testament tell us that Jesus and his disciples attended a feast on the evening before his Crucifixion. There are differences in the accounts of the Gospels, but all of them recount that Jesus told his disciples to eat bread and drink wine and that the bread was his flesh and the wine, his blood. Two accounts also note that Jesus instructed them to do so in the future, in his memory. The feast at which Jesus dined with his disciples took place close to the Passover sacrifice in the Temple, and some believe that it was a Passover Seder.

Since then, one of the most important sacraments in the Catholic Church is the Mass, or Eucharist, which means gratitude or grace. During this ceremony, the priest or cardinal replicates the act of Jesus, who served bread and wine to his disciples. He recites the appropriate verses and distributes bread and wine to the faithful. It is believed that, during this ceremony, the wine becomes the blood of Jesus and the bread—his flesh. The bread used for the Mass is made from wheat and, in the Western church, does not include yeast to avoid crumbs after its dedication. The Western Catholic Church uses small round wafers instead of real bread. The wine used is always alcoholic wine made from grapes without additives. It can be red or white.

I will not go into the details of the ceremony here, but just note that it is a reenactment of the "Lord's Supper." It is as though the participants dine with the Lord, and the ceremony is often called thus. The wine (the blood) and the bread (the flesh) are sacrificed to the father through the son. The ceremony is apparently reminiscent of the sacrificial ceremony that took place in the Temple before its destruction.

The priest conducting the Eucharist arranges the altar and places on it cups of wine and utensils for the holy bread. A vessel of wine, a vessel of water, and a Mass book are also displayed. In festive Masses, the bread and wine are brought to the altar in a ritual procession. Festive Masses also occasionally use incense, which is produced from a wood resin placed on charcoal in a special container. The incense symbolically sanctifies the objects and the people over whom it is censed. After reciting the Eucharist and Holy Communion prayers, the priest blesses the bread, eats of it, and sips the wine. The congregation then approaches in line or several lines to receive the bread in the form of a wafer served straight into the mouth. The wafer is eaten immediately. It is often possible also to sip the wine or dip the wafer in the wine before eating it.

Attributes of Basic Flavors	
Flavor / Aroma	Definition
Sour	Lemony flavor
Pungent	Sensation of acidity
Salty	Literally tastes similar to salt
Bitter	A bitter flavor, such as bittersweet chocolate
Sweet	Basic flavor similar to sugar
Sticky	Texture that sticks to teeth or palate
Fatty	Fatty taste, such as butter or cream
Creamy	Like cream filling in a layer cake
Fruity	Aroma of any fruit, yellow, white, or red
Woody	Aroma of wood from the barrel in which the wine was stored
Mushroom	Aroma of forest, mildew, fresh mushrooms
Lactic	Aroma of yogurt, milk, cream, fresh butter
Spicy	Aroma of black pepper, cinnamon, mint, etc.
Toasted	Aroma of toasted bread, coffee, chicory, etc.

This table describes the flavors and aromas that wine experts use when writing articles in magazines that deal with wine. In reality, there are other fragrances, and the existing fragrances can also be divided into subtypes, but this is a matter for experts who can, for example, distinguish between the taste of strawberries and the taste of raspberries or blueberries. However, the regular consumer is not an expert and the categorization in the above table seems sufficient.

Chapter Three

BEER IS EVERYWHERE

1. The Agricultural Revolution

Yuval Noah Harari writes[1] that the First Agricultural Revolution began in the Middle East some ten thousand years ago. At that time, humans began to grow several species of plants and to domesticate animals. It was a long process during which wheat, and later peas and lentils, was developed as a crop. Wheat and similar plants became basic human food and contributed to population growth. Wheat farming contributed to the creation of urban settlements. Around 8500 BCE, when fields of domesticated wheat were beginning to be cultivated, Jericho's oasis supported a town with a population of one thousand. Yuval Noah Harari clarifies that the agricultural revolution was in fact a slow and gradual process that took thousands of years.

The constant cultivation of wheat in the Middle East created permanent settlements—villages—and the more food people had, the more children were born in each generation. When cities began to be formed, the mechanisms of cooperation among the inhabitants became more sophisticated, and the Sumerian script, written on signs scratched on wet clay panels, was created. At first, they recorded product definitions and quantities, and over the years, additional signs were added that gradually turned the

---

1   Yuval Noah Harari, *Sapiens: A Brief History of Humankind* (Tel Aviv-Yafo: Kinneret Zmora Bitan Dvir, 2011).

symbols into written language. Between 3000 and 2500 BCE the Sumerian symbols became a full script, known as the "cuneiform script." At the same time, a full script called "hieroglyphics" was being developed in ancient Egypt. It is not yet known whether the two scripts were independently invented or whether there was a connection between them as they were developed.

The first cities were established in Mesopotamia, between the Euphrates and Tigris Rivers, in an area that is today part of Iraq. The urban residents were, for the most part, farmers who went to work in their fields every morning, but there were also craftsmen and municipal administrators. There were also religious leaders who held religious ceremonies during the holidays. Reasons for this urbanization are still being researched. People may have wanted to live close to a religious center, perhaps it was a desire to be near a commercial center, and there could also have been a security reason, as a walled city protected its inhabitants from occasional enemies.

Around 3000 BCE, Uruk was the largest city in Mesopotamia. It was inhabited by close to three thousand people, and its culti-vated, irrigated fields surrounded it for up to ten kilometers from the city itself. By 2000 BCE most of the inhabitants of Mesopo-tamia lived in large cities belonging to several "kingdoms."[2]

The two great civilizations in antiquity were Egypt on the banks of the Nile and Mesopotamia on the banks of the Euphrates and Tigris. We will not discuss the political aspects here; we will be content with the fact that these cultures were created thanks to the surplus of agricultural products, especially surplus grains, which

---

2   The main kingdoms were Uruk, Ur, Lagash, Eridu, and Nippur.

established a class of administrators and enabled public works, such as irrigation canals, paved streets, temples, and palaces.

2. What Did They Drink in Mesopotamia and Egypt?

As noted above, written symbols developed initially as a method for collecting economic data. It was necessary to record who provided which product to whom. Thus we know that in the cities of Sumer, residents consumed quantities of wheat, barley, lamb meat, and cloth. Tax records, given in kind (i.e., products and services), have made this clear. There were also warehouses that kept surplus wheat and barley, dates, onions, beans, and lentils.

The tablet writing of the Sumerians evolved into a rich language in which great sagas were written. The most famous of these is the *Epic of Gilgamesh*. Gilgamesh was a king of Sumer who ruled around 2700 BCE, but over the years his story was also accepted in the kingdoms of Akkad and Babylon, both established after Sumer. The epic describes the plots of Gilgamesh and his friend Enkidu. To sample the story, we will make do with a small passage in which Enkidu—who was a wild man—runs naked in the field and meets a young woman. She takes him into a shepherd's house in a village with a sophisticated population, serves him bread and beer, and urges him to drink the beer, the beverage of their village. Enkidu ate the bread and drank seven mugs of beer and was very pleased. His face shone with great joy.

Enkidu did not know about bread and beer; he was a wild man. But from the text we learn that during the days of Gilgamesh, they drank beer in Uruk, and in the eyes of the people, bread and beer were what distinguished civilized people from wild people. The epic also shows that drunkenness by drinking beer was a familiar phenomenon and absolutely not ruled out. The wonders of bread and beer, and also wine, were acceptable in Sumer. Writings from the beginning of the fifth dynasty in Egypt, dating back to 2350 BCE, indicate that beer was a common drink in ancient Egypt as well. Beer was called *hert* and is mentioned often. It also had religious significance, and one of the goddesses, Hath, was the goddess of beer.[3]

In ancient Egypt, drunkenness was treated with severity. In bookkeeping manuals (there was such a profession in Egypt) it is explicitly stated that drunkenness was forbidden and that it did not represent the values of Egyptian society. Drinking beer was fine, but in moderate amounts. In both Egypt and Sumer, it was believed that the gods had given beer to the people to be used in religious and social ceremonies. In both societies, beer was acceptable at important events and was consumed by kings, aristocracy, and commoners.

In Egypt and Mesopotamia, grains and other products were subject to taxation. Part of the harvest was pledged to the temple and then distributed to artisans and laborers who built public projects. Goods were used as a substitute for money in the sense that they could be taxed or given as wages. In Mesopotamia, temple workers received part of their wages in the form of a liter of beer a day. More important workers received a larger amount.

Beer was part of the traditional wedding gift given by the groom's father to the bride's family. Soldiers and police also received beer jugs as part of their wages, as well as raw barley and clothes. Each such transaction was recorded on small clay tablets.

---

3   For more see Samuel N. Cramer, *History Begins at Sumer* (London: Themes and Hudson, 1961); Bruce G. Trigger, *Understanding Early Civilizations: A Comparative Study* (Cambridge, MA: Cambridge University Press, 2003).

In Egypt, around 2500 BCE, the builders of the pyramids received part of their wages in the form of beer jars and loaves of bread. Written evidence shows that the builders of the pyramids were not slaves but hired employees. The state collected wheat as a tax and distributed the "collection" (some of which was processed) to its employees as wages in the form of bread and beer.

A cuneiform tablet from 2100 BCE, from the Sumerian city of Nippur, describes a list of medicinal products based on beer and alcohol, as well as perfumes and spices, such as onion juice, garlic flakes, and dried olives. In Egypt, too, there were medicines of this kind. Incidentally, alcohol is better than water as a basis for medication because it destroys bacteria. Also, in Egypt it was customary to bury the dead with beer jars, so that they would have a proper drink on their long journey to the afterlife.

3. What Do You Drink with a Straw?

We don't know when people from Mesopotamia and Egypt began to make beer from grains. It is estimated that in 4000 BCE, beer was a familiar and favorite drink. An archaeological discovery (pictogram) of the same period depicts two figures drinking beer from a large jug by using a drinking straw that is probably made of reeds. The beer that was produced was then mixed with seeds of grain, straw flakes, and other solids, and reed straws were necessary to avoid swallowing them. From 3300 BCE there is already written evidence that beer was a well-known drink in Mesopotamia.

There was a great advantage to seeds of grains, wheat, and barley: they could be stored for long periods, and if desired, they could be cooked in a stew or porridge. This was not an easy task because of the need to heat water, but it was a significant addition to the vegetable diet of those days. Over time, it turned out that grains had another advantage: when you soak grains in water, they begin to germinate, and malt is created, which can be used to sweeten liquids. Today we know that the sweetness is created by enzymes that form starch and later sugar. In those days it was almost the only source of sugar, because bee honey was rare and expensive.

Another discovery, in those ancient days, was that if you let the mixture of grain and water sit for a few more days, a sparkling beverage with alcohol was created. Alcohol is also made from the fermentation of fruits, especially grapes, which have a high natural sugar content. But the production of alcohol from grain was cheaper. In time, as they learned more about the fermentation process, they understood that adding the malt produced more sugar and heating increased the production of alcohol from the starch found in the grains. Those involved in the refining process also learned that reusing the jars had another advantage, which stems from the yeast cultures that attach themselves to the sides and in the grooves of the vessel. Ultimately, they understood that occasionally adding strawberries or spices to the mix improved the taste of the drink. Documents from 2000 BCE mention about twenty types of beer that were classified by color (dark or light), alcohol levels, and taste strength.

Beer also contributed to the social sphere, and it was a common beverage at social events. In the second millennium BCE, beer was perceived as the gift of the gods and had religious value as well. And of course, it also had economic value. Anthropologists have believed for years that it was a significant factor in the expansion of grain crops in ancient times. In this matter, there is disagreement, as not all experts attribute such importance to the foamy drink.

4. Beer in the Middle Ages and in the Modern Era

The Greek historian Polybius related that the industry of beer production came to ancient Greece from Egypt with the help of the Phoenicians, who traded with both countries. Another version supports direct imports from Egypt to Greece. Either way, the Greeks learned to make beer from barley, and this custom spread to Rome. For the Roman nobility, however, the preferred drink was water mixed with wine.

Beer was a common drink in ancient Greece and Rome. The Roman historian Tacitus noted that German tribes who lived outside the empire used to drink beer. The tradition of drinking beer was maintained even after the fall of the Roman Empire. In the Middle Ages there were "guilds" of beer manufacturers, and, as was customary, they had a Christian saint who represented them and watched over them in Germany and Belgium. The Frankish emperor Charlemagne, as well as his heirs, recognized the importance of the beverage. The Franks also drank wine, though it was more expensive than beer. Beer was consumed mainly by the commoners.

St. Benedict (480–547 CE) founded the monasteries in Western Europe. He determined rules for convent behavior, as well as standards for performing tasks. Apart from prayers, the monks had to help travelers and passengers on the roads and give them food and drink. As a rule, the monasteries would produce all their own food. The most common drink was beer, and a glass of beer was served at breakfast. Later, this practice became popular in the general public, and Queen Elizabeth I used to complete breakfast with a glass of beer.

Fernand Braudel notes[4] that, during the Middle Ages, Europe was divided into drinking areas: the north was "the land of beer," and the south was considered "the land of wine." At the beginning of the Middle Ages, beer drinking was widespread primarily in Scandinavia and Germany, but over the years it spread to the lower altitude countries. At the same time, beer became a drink acceptable to the general population, and the demand for beer increased throughout Europe.

The main technological improvement in the Middle Ages was the addition of hops to the production of beer. This addition was noted in the ninth century, beginning in 822 CE. Beer based on hops, in addition to grain, was considered preferable and had a longer shelf life. Further improvements in beer production were added in the thirteenth century in Bohemia. As a result of its longer shelf life, it was possible to transfer beer from place to place, although not for long distances.

In the sixteenth century, taverns were social institutions where drunkenness was commonplace. At night the streets of the large cities in Europe were filled with drunken patrons staggering through the mud, and there was strong social criticism. But beer was not only a means of drunken celebration, it was also the second most important source of nutrition after bread. Housewives baked bread and cooked beer every few days. In her book,[5] Toni Mount

---

4   Fernand Braudel, *Civilization and Capitalism, 15th–18th Century,* vol. 2, *The Wheels of Commerce* (New York: Harper & Row Publishers, 1982).

5   Toni Mount, *Everyday Life in Medieval London: From the Anglo-Saxons to the Tudors* (Gloucestershire: Amberley Publishing, 2015).

describes in detail the social context and how people bought beer from neighbors who made it. Since unpasteurized beer tends to go sour, neighbors would take turns making the beer. Every few days, one of them would prepare beer and the neighbors would buy it. Since the water was not pure or safe for use in the big cities, the workers would take "beer breaks" in the morning and, of course, drink beer with dinner too.

At the end of the Middle Ages and the beginning of the modern era, almost every beverage contained alcohol in some measure, and drunkenness took a heavy toll. There were drunken physicians, drunken generals, drunken popes, and princes with the tremors every morning. It is not surprising, then, that reducing drinking was one of the first of Martin Luther's goals when he set out to reform the Church. During that time the First League was established, to help people abstain from drinking. This was a group of upper-class Germans inspired by Luther, and the group members voluntarily restricted themselves to seven glasses of beer per meal.

Beer production in England was subject to strict supervision. There was a distinction between beer and ale (beer made without hops), and each was made by a separate guild. In every country, beer production was recognized as an important profession, and over time, the volume of production increased and the price dropped due to the efficiency of production in large series. Consumption also increased because of this. In the fifteenth century, firms in Germany produced an average of three hundred liters a year. At the beginning of the seventeenth century, the average quantity produced by a single manufacturer was seven thousand liters.

The use of hops spread in the Netherlands and England as early as the fifteenth century. When beer became a common beverage, government supervision increased, clarity and filtering rules were applied, and the basic components were occasionally redefined. At the same time, the authorities imposed a tax on drinks containing alcohol. In Belgium, for example, a heavy tax was imposed on French wines, which gave impetus to the local production of beer. To this day, the Belgians excel in both production and consumption of the fermented grain drink.

5. Innovations in Beer Production in Modern Times

At the beginning of the modern era, it was clear that there were different customs when it came to the consumption of beer. On the one hand, Germans and Central Europeans preferred a cold beer that they would store in caves in the high mountains. On the other hand, England had a clear preference for drinking beer at room temperature, and it was stored in the cellars. In the Middle Ages, beer was produced in small quantities by households. Later on, various manufacturers began to produce beer in larger quantities. In 1295, King Wenceslaus II granted production rights to the town of Pilsen in Bohemia, and in time, additional guilds in Germany also gained the rights to produce beer.

In 1516, German authorities began to set standards for the production of beer, which gave them the advantage of large-scale production. In 1553, a firm by the name of Beck was established, which produces delicious beer to this day. Later, in 1602, beer began to be sold in glass bottles with a cork (like wine). Beer production also spread to North America, and in 1674, Harvard College began to produce beer independently. Another famous figure was William Penn, who founded the State of Pennsylvania in the United States but was previously a manufacturer and supplier of beer commercially. We can also mention George Washington, who wrote a recipe for home beer in 1757. A short time later, in 1786, the Molson brewery was established in Canada, and it exists to this day.

In the nineteenth century, beer production became a real industry. In the 1850s, several German beer manufacturers migrated to the United States—their last names were Anheuser, Miller, Coors, Stroh, and Schlitz. Beer production improved, as did distribution methods. The railways transported beer bottles to the country's peripheries in special caravans. Pasteurization techniques from 1876 onwards enabled a long shelf life and aided in the distribution of beer. In 1890, Pabst was the first brewery in the United States to sell more than a million bottles in a year.

Prohibition laws in the United States affected the beer industry as it had affected the wine industry. In 1914, there were 1,400 breweries in the United States, and when the ban on alcohol ended in 1933, only 160 beer producers remained. In 1935, the US began to package beer in cans, and Mrs. Aliza Miller, who ran Miller's brewery, used them to improve cooling. Metal cooling was easier than glass cooling. During the twentieth century, beer production expanded both in Europe and the US, and in 1990, the United States produced about 20 percent of the world's beer. By the end of the twentieth century, the world's drinkers consumed 5.9 billion gallons of beer. In the United States alone, sales reached $46 billion at the century's end.

6. Beer Production Today

Today beer is produced in almost every country. Supply has grown every year, and on supermarket shelves there are dozens of beautiful bottles with attractive labels. There are review columns in the written press, where experts pen stylized descriptions to detail the characteristics of the drink. We can read about conflicting and complementary flavors, the body of the drink, the carbonation (the bubbles rising from the bottom of the glass), and the foam above. We can also read about the aroma, because malt contributes aromas of bread, sugar, walnut, and caramel; and, experts say, hops contribute aromas of flowers, fruits, herbs, and citrus. The taste of roasting plays an important role in experts' opinions. Some speak of refreshing bitterness and bitter sweetness at different levels. Moreover, the columns cover suggestions for successful combinations of beer and food, just like wine.

So how is beer made, and what goes into this golden alcoholic beverage (usually)? The production ingredients of the finished product are water, alcohol (3–5 percent), sugar (0.5 percent), protein (0.5 percent), and carbon dioxide (0.25 percent). The production process is fairly simple, but it has many variations. To prepare beer, start with barley or wheat seeds, which, after proper treatment, become malt.

In the **first stage**, barley is soaked in regular water and allowed to germinate at an average temperature of fourteen–eighteen degrees Celsius. Today, this is done while oxygen flows through and constantly mixes the barley. During germination, enzymes are released from the seeds, turning the hard matter inside the nucleus into soluble sugars. Within two days, the seed loses its hardness and the bud sprouts and roots grow out.

In the **second stage**, it is customary to stop the germination by a process called "drying" or "roasting," and so that the flavor components do not pass to the developing stem, the barley kernel is separated from the sprout. The degree of roasting determines the color of the seed and the color of the resulting beer. The drying, in suitable ovens, determines the basic taste of the beer. Drying at low temperatures does no damage to the living enzymes, and they will be used later on. Drying at high temperatures causes some of the sugar to turn into caramel, which contributes a number of other flavors, especially the taste of nuts and coffee (experts believe). At the end of this stage we have the "malt" barley, which is the sole source of sugar and alcohol in the drink (for example, in the beers of Heineken and Carlsberg). But some manufacturers add other types of grains during the fermentation period, such as extra rice in US-made Budweiser beer.

The **third stage** is cooking. The malt, which contains the base materials, is shredded, ground, and transferred to a primary cooking tank. Hot water is added to this container and stirred to produce the mixture called the mash. At this stage, the amount of sugars in the mash is determined by the cooking temperature.

In the **fourth stage**, the mixture is filtered and diluted, and transferred to large cooking containers. In this stage, hops are added in fixed portions throughout the cooking time; they add bitterness to the liquid.

In the **fifth stage**, the cooked liquid is refrigerated in fermentation tanks, and when it reaches a suitable temperature, yeast is added. The yeast turns sugar into alcohol and carbon dioxide. In this process, white foam is formed on the surface of the liquid. The fermentation lasts eight to ten days, and at the end, it is raw beer.

In the **sixth stage**, the raw beer is transferred to a maturation tank, where the temperature is low and sometimes close to freezing level. The maturation time can last several weeks. At this point carbon dioxide and other liquids and yeast may be added. The duration of this stage depends on the type of beer. Ale is cooked for only a few days at higher temperatures. Stout cooks longer and contains a higher percentage of alcohol.

In the **seventh stage**, liquids and gas are mixed at a low temperature (just above freezing) and transferred to barrels, bottles, and cans. Beer in metal cans and glass bottles is pasteurized in the container by gradually heating to sixty-two degrees Celsius for half an hour, and at the end of the process, it undergoes additional chilling. Beer intended for storage in barrels undergoes very rapid heating to destroy bacteria and then is cooled again and poured into metal barrels. Draft beer should be "fresher" than bottled beer, and it tastes milder.

7. Cider

Cider is an alcoholic beverage made from apples. You can find it on stores shelves near the beer. Like beer, this beverage also has a modest alcohol component of 4–6 percent. This is a refreshing and slightly sour drink that also has an interesting history.

It is unknown who invented cider and when. Information on its existence is known from the books of the Roman historian Pliny (23–79 CE), in which he describes it without saying when and where it was first created. In the first century CE, cider was imbibed in relatively moderate quantities in comparison to beer and wine. After the fall of Rome, cider continued to be produced and drunk in the western part of the empire. What we know about the creation of the drink in the late Middle Ages is that it came to Normandy (France) from Cordova scientists in the tenth century CE. As detailed in the chapter on alcohol, Andalusian scientists pioneered the production of alcohol from various plants, including apples. Their knowledge spread to the south and west of France, and when Normandy connected to England via a "personal union ship" in the eleventh century, cider also arrived in England.

By the tenth century, cider production was considered a prominent agricultural industry in France and Spain. But it was not until the twelfth century that its development progressed through changing the tree species and by improving the technique for extracting the fluid from the fruit. Beginning in 1212, there are documents attesting to the production of cider in English monasteries. In the reign of Edward I (1274–1307), cider was also a source of income for the monarchy when a tax was imposed. However, cider production became a leading agricultural industry in the seventeenth century. The production consisted of two stages: In the first stage, the juice was squeezed and transferred for fermentation. The result was a drink with a taste of apples in which the amount of alcohol was felt.[6] In the second stage, water was added to the pulp of the remaining apples, and from there a diluted cider, called "small cyder," with a small amount of alcohol, was produced. The weakness of the "small cyder" made it easy to spoil, so they added spices and boiled it to prolong its shelf life.

Cider production was carried out in the farmers' homes. Because of the alcohol, the drink could be kept for several months by storing it in cool cellars. The drink was then delivered for consumption in cities in large barrels.

It is important to note that in order to produce large amounts of apple juice, suitable apple varieties that have a high juice component are required. The problem is that investment in fruit trees reaches fruition within seven to ten years when a tended plantation produces large quantities of fruit. The economic viability depends on the price of cider in the market and the price of the

---

6   Studies from this period put the amount of alcohol in the primary cider (base) at 4.16 percent, as reported by R. K. French, 1982.

apples themselves, which can be sold in the markets for "table consumption." During the seventeenth century it was worthwhile to produce a first cider that sold well at a high price in large cities and especially in London. At the same time, the "weak cider" sold in the local market as a simple drink.

Towards the end of the eighteenth century, "first cider" became less worthwhile for farmers because the price did not cover all the expenses.[7] Although the cider was considered a delicious drink, the price was too high to capture a large market share. At the end of the eighteenth century there were fluctuations in the price of "high cider" sold in London and a lot of customers simply avoided drinking it. As a result, farmers stopped planting new apple trees and in fact neglected their existing orchards. The existing plantations of red apple trees (Redstreak) managed to produce edible fruit, which was then fashionable as healthy food. This is also when the famous saying "An apple a day keeps the doctor away" came into use, used as marketing for fresh apples. During the nineteenth century, the price of European wine fell, and the cider branch never returned to its former days of greatness. Cider in France and the UK is still produced today and can be found near the beer shelf of every supermarket. This is an excellent, delicious, and nutritious beverage, but public tastes have pushed it to secondary status.

---

7   There was a period in the eighteenth century where part of the wages of production workers in the apple industry was paid in the form of cider, similar to the situation regarding beer that was customary in antiquity in Egypt and discussed at the beginning of the chapter.

Main Types of Beer

Lager: Beer produced by a "bottom fermentation" process of yeast and stored for several weeks in cooled cellars for clarification and aging. It has a bright color and high carbonation. Most of the beers in the world are of this type.

Ale: Beer produced by the process of "upper fermentation," as in ancient times. It has a heavy body and dark color. The alcohol content is high, and there is lower carbonation.

Pilsner: A light beer characterized by a strong taste of hops. It originated in the city of Pilsen, formerly in Bohemia and today in the Czech Republic.

Stout: A heavy beer and "body" with a high alcohol content. Its color is dark, and it has a slightly sweet taste. (Porter beer is essentially weak stout.)

Bitter: A form of ale but "dry," containing a high percentage of alcohol.

Bock: A dark, rich, and heavy beer, usually made in early spring and sold at the end of the summer.

Chapter Four

ALCOHOL—
THE BEVERAGE OF LIFE

1. Muslim Science in Southern Spain

The city of Córdoba in Andalusia in southern Spain lies on the banks of the Guadalquivir River at the foot of the Sierra Morena Mountains. The city is built in Arab style and has beautiful buildings from the Arab period, the most famous of which is the Mezquita—the Great Mosque. Córdoba was the capital of the Umayyad rulers of Spain (756–1031 CE) and an important center of cultural life, art, and science. In the tenth century, before the end of the first millennium, Córdoba was one of the most important cities in Europe. The city was then under enlightened Muslim rule, and the public administration functioned well. There were palaces, parks, and paved roads in the city, and the main streets were lit at night by oil lamps. There were numerous mosques, dozens of public bathhouses, and a functioning sewage system. In the tenth century it had a central library, containing almost half a million books (a particularly large number for a library at the end of the first millennium). Córdoba, the birthplace of Maimonides, was also an important city in Jewish culture.

During this period, Muslims ruled from southern Spain, through North Africa to the Middle East, and even beyond to Central Asia. Muslims had learned mathematics, philosophy, and applied algebra from the Greeks. The numerical system we use to this day is called "Arabic numerals" (although it originated in

India). During this period, the Arabs were active mariners who used navigational aids that were well advanced for their time. They used plant extracts to anesthetize patients and even contributed to the development of chemical methods for distillation.

Jabir ibn Hayyan (721–815 CE), a ninth-century founder of the science of chemistry, described in detail methods of distilling wine and other liquids. Muslim researchers in Spain improved his methods and used them mainly to produce fragrance extracts. In their research, they even turned saltwater into fresh water, and among other experiments, they distilled wine.

Distillation made wine "strong." In other words, it increased the percentage of alcohol contained in it. This is because alcohol evaporates at seventy-eight degrees Celsius and water evaporates at one hundred degrees Celsius. Slow heating of wine causes evaporation, the steam is transferred through a pipe from one copper container (the heating tool) to another vessel (the target vessel), and when it thickens at a lower temperature, the liquid in the target vessel remains with a higher alcohol component. The process does not produce pure alcohol but rather "fortified wine" with a significantly higher alcohol content. This Arab innovation was later passed on to Christian Europe, and there, too, experiments were conducted in the distillation and production of "fortified" wine, later called "burnt wine."

The Italians in the twelfth century continued the alcohol distillation process. They learned about it from books written in Arabic; they experimented with distillation and found that lighting an alcoholic liquid generated intense combustion. They also discussed the results of drinking the liquid: at first it creates a burning feeling in the esophagus and stomach and some degree of discomfort, but then it is followed by a pleasant, light sensation.

The first use of the distilled drink was for medical purposes. The French scholar Arnald de Villanova, at the Montpellier Medical School in the fourteenth century, called a drink that was created after three levels of distillation "*aqua vitae*"—the water of life—and elaborated on its medicinal effect.

Villanova and his students believed that alcohol could prolong human life up to the age of seventy years, a relatively rare and honorable age during this period. Medical records that have survived from the fourteenth century indicate that a distilled alcoholic drink was credited, along with extending life expectancy, with relieving pain, and especially reducing toothaches. Physicians of the period believed that this drink was also good in preventing fragmented speech and in preventing paralysis, and that it was also effective against the epidemics common in those days. In the fifteenth century, the new drink was recognized as beneficial even outside the medical world, and its use became popular. Michael Puff von Schrick of Augsburg published a widely circulated medical book in 1478 (with fourteen editions by 1500), in which he recommended a "spoonful of alcohol drink" every morning for good health and prevention of various diseases.

2. Alcoholic Drinks: Grease for the Wheels of the Slave Trade

During the fifteenth century, alcohol was also recommended for nonmedicinal uses and began to be consumed in large quantities, mainly in northern Europe. The Gaelic term for the water of life was *uisge beatha*, a word combination that is the source of the word *whiskey*. In other countries, and especially in Germany, it was called burnt wine (originally in German *brandewijn*). In Yiddish, the term for burnt wine (*yeyn saraf*) was shortened to the acronym "yash." The term "burnt wine" was also recorded in several countries as "brandywine" and in short "brandy," and the term was used in the language spoken at the time.

In the fifteenth century, geographical discoveries became the focus and passion of the Christian rulers of Europe. The forerunner of this age of discovery was Portuguese Prince Henry the Navigator, the third son of King João (1385–1433). Henry himself only left Portugal three times, for short trips to North Africa. But from his base in Sagres, in southern Portugal, he invested the kingdom's money in extensive expeditions to West Africa and the Atlantic Ocean. He financed sea voyages and collected, documented, and edited the reports their commanders gave him. He encouraged the sea captains to use advanced navigational instruments, including a magnetic compass and an astrolabe, tools used by Arab sailors decades earlier. The economic motive for the voyages of maritime discovery in the fifteenth century was the hope of reaching eastern India, thus opening a new channel for the spice trade, which until then had been controlled by the Arabs in the Middle East.

The Arabs in the Middle East were also knowledgeable about growing sugarcane. From the beginning of the second millennium, they used irrigation channels and pumped water from wells using a manual screw pump. In order to grow their sugarcane, they did not hesitate to use slaves from eastern Africa. Europeans were familiar with sugarcane from the time of the Crusades, but they had not succeeded in growing it in Europe. Europeans also had no source of slaves after the destruction of the Roman Empire in the fifth century CE, and Christian doctrine forbade the slavery of Christians. The number of non-Christian slaves from Eastern Europe was limited. Indeed, there were Muslim prisoners of war in Christian Europe, but the policy was to convert them to save their lost souls from the chains of Muslim doctrine.

The Atlantic islands that were controlled by Portugal—Madeira, the Azores, and the Canaries—had a climate suitable for cultivating sugarcane. The sailors sent by the Kingdom of Portugal to explore the shores of West Africa occasionally purchased local slaves and brought them to these islands for the purpose of growing sugarcane. These slaves were neither Christians nor considered by the Europeans to be potential converts, and as pagans they were subjected to slavery without remorse. This practice of importing slaves from West Africa to the Canary Islands was later used to establish slavery for economic reasons in the Americas.

In the Caribbean islands, discovered by Columbus in 1492, there was no gold, but Columbus understood that the land was suitable for growing sugarcane. In 1493, on his second trip to the Caribbean, he took cuttings of sugarcane for planting. And the rest (as cliché lovers say) is history. In order to grow sugarcane, a great deal of manpower was needed. The native "Indians" living in America were not suited for this work, and great numbers of them were dying of diseases brought by European settlers. The solution was to acquire slaves from West Africa and bring them to the New World. Over the next 350 years, eleven million Africans were brought to this New World controlled by the Spanish, the Portuguese, the French, and the English. Two-way international trade was created: slaves were brought to various American countries, and the sugar produced in those American countries was sold in Europe at a high price.

But what is the connection between the slave trade and alcoholic beverages? Simply put, shortly after the slave trade became institutionalized, it became clear that local slave traders in West

Africa were very fond of European wine and even more of liquor. Alcoholic beverages, high in alcohol, turned out to be better than wine, which could go bad on ships sailing for several weeks from Europe to Africa in the summer. Brandy, which had a higher alcohol content, did not spoil, and because it was consumed in smaller quantities than wine, it required less storage space. So alcoholic beverages were used as currency in the slave trade, along with textiles and metal products.

The African name for European brandy was *dashee*, and it became the grease for the wheels of slave trade. The boatmen who carried slaves from the coast to the European ships received part of their wages in bottles of brandy. The connection between brandy and slaves grew even stronger when the European settlers learned to produce alcoholic beverages from crushed sugarcane.

3. Sugar and Rum in the Caribbean Sea

At the beginning of the seventeenth century, English colonization began. The annexation of colonies to the British throne began under the reign of Elizabeth I. The colony of Virginia in North America was named after her (Queen Elizabeth I was called The Virgin Queen). In the first quarter of the century, English settlers founded several colonies in North America and the Caribbean. In 1627, English settlers also arrived in Barbados, an island that was almost uninhabited. At first they tried to grow tobacco, a product greatly favored by people in England. But the local conditions were not right, and the tobacco was a much lower quality than the tobacco grown in Virginia. For this reason, the Brazilian settlers imported sugarcane, a crop that was much more suited to the local climate. In Cuba—one of the Caribbean islands—sugarcane is grown to this day.

The sugar industry was dependent on cheap labor, and slaves were brought from West Africa. The use of workers in slavery conditions was permitted by the Christian church. Plantation owners in Barbados and elsewhere had learned from the Portuguese residents of Brazil to produce an alcoholic beverage from crushed sugarcane. The Portuguese used the foam that formed on the surface of the bubbling liquid, which later formed the solid sugar. The people of Barbados improved the process and used the thick liquid remaining after sugar production, called molasses, which had enough sugar to extract alcohol. The new drink was initially called "rumbullion" and later was shortened to "rum." At first, the drink was sold to the plantation owners, who gave it to slaves in generous quantities, and later it was sold to ships anchored off the island's shores.

Rum became popular among the sailors of the British naval fleet anchored in the Caribbean Sea. Local rum had an advantage over beer and wine, which had to be brought from Europe and tended to spoil on the long journey. Rum, like any alcoholic liquor, does not spoil in long storage and requires little storage space. In the 1740s, Admiral Edward Vernon, the commander of the British Caribbean Navy, ordered a mix of rum with two servings of water and, to improve the taste of the drink, added sugar (which was abundant) and lime juice (also in copious supply). And so the first cocktail was invented. The sailors, who called their commander Old Grog (the word *grog* derived from the type of fabric of Vernon's jackets), called the new drink after him: grog. Thus Vernon's name was commemorated for generations without his ever winning important naval battles.

The use of grog instead of beer became an integral part of the diet for the sailors of the English Navy. It also had a side benefit, because the lime mixed with grog contained (as does all citrus) vitamin C, which reduced the incidence of scurvy. The change from beer to grog made the British Navy sailors healthier. Grog also became popular due to its easy preservation, and within a short time it became an international alcoholic drink.

4. Cocktails

Grog was a mixture of basic alcohol (rum), water, sugar, and fruit juices. Within a few decades, the practice of mixing a few drinks together became common, and all such mixtures were given the name "cocktail," or "rooster tail." According to the American dictionary Merriam-Webster: "A cocktail is a usually iced drink of wine or distilled liquor mixed with flavoring ingredients." One of the first cocktail recipes was published in 1831 by a British officer of Scottish origin, James Edward Alexander. Alexander described his cocktail as "a mixture of one-third of an alcoholic beverage, such as brandy, gin or rum, and two-thirds of water, ice or fruit juice, and enriched with sugar and spices."

There is a debate over the origin of the name "cocktail" for this drink, but it is agreed among researchers that by 1806 the term was commonly used in newspapers of the period. Some theories attempt to explain the origin of the name. The **first explanation** relates to a corruption of the French word *coquetier*, literally "egg cup." This refers to a small cup with a rooster tail–shaped handle. The name was adopted because a pharmacy owner in New Orleans introduced his customers to a mixture of brandy and herbs in such cups at the end of the eighteenth century. The mixture was considered a medication at the time and was mixed into small glasses. A **second explanation** is based on the word *tailing* in the sense of "following." When beer barrels in inns were almost empty and the beer that remained at the bottom was not as good, they improved it by adding fruit juice. The tap at the bottom of the beer barrels was rudely dubbed *cock*. Hence the linguistic interpretation: the subsequent drink, that is, what was below the tap level at the bottom of the barrel, was called the cocktail. A **third explanation** is that simple horses had a high tail resembling the tail of a rooster, and racehorses known as thoroughbreds had a non-rising tail. Occasionally non-purebred horses would be introduced into the races, identified by their rising tails. From this, cocktail became the name of non-pure alcoholic beverages—that is, alcohol mixed with other ingredients. **Yet another explanation** is that the colors of most cocktails (mainly yellowish white) are similar to the feather colors in the tail of a rooster.

In the nineteenth century, dozens of mixtures were produced, some of which were collated in Jerry Thomas's 1862 book, *How to Mix Drinks*.[1] Thomas was called "professor" but actually was a bartender who systematically tried various blends, which he submitted to his guests and then recorded their reactions. His book summarized the knowledge of his time in this field. He included ten alcoholic beverages and a detailed explanation of how to prepare them, step-by-step. Over time, specific glasses were determined for each drink. For example, the drink called a highball is actually whiskey mixed with soda and is named after the tall glass in which it is served. I should also mention a Mrs. Walsh, who hosted the first cocktail party in St. Louis in May of 1917. The newspaper headline covering the party heralded "The Newest Stunt in Society: The Cocktail Party."

---

1   Jerry Thomas, *Jerry Thomas Bartenders Guide: How to Mix All Kinds of Plain and Fancy Drinks* (Mineola, NY: Dover Publications, 2016; first ed. 1862).

In the chapter about wine, we covered the ban on the production and sale of alcohol in the United States between 1920 and 1933. During this period, the use of homemade cocktails increased in taverns. These were alcoholic drinks made under improvised conditions, earning them names like moonshine whiskey or bathtub gin. They were not of high quality and their taste was not like the real drink, but when they were mixed with fruit juice it was possible to enjoy them. In Miami, for example, there was a drink called the "bees knees," which was homemade gin mixed with lemon juice and honey, making it palatable.

The demand for cocktails during these years was particularly high. Al Capone, one of the top mafia leaders in the United States, ran the Chicago liquor distribution network, and earned $60 million from the liquor business, according to press reports. (He was finally arrested for income tax evasion, not for illegal alcohol trafficking, because there was not enough evidence to convict him of the latter.) Prohibition laws prevented tax revenues on alcoholic beverages. The loss of tax revenues was estimated at close to $1 billion per year.

5. The Dangers of Excessive Drinking

Overdrinking of intoxicating beverages of the type described in this chapter creates addiction. Many books document the scope of alcoholism and its damage. Alcohol abuse accounts for more than 3 percent of all deaths, and even before that, alcohol causes extensive health damage. On the one hand, we have the sense that alcohol is a common ingredient in parties, celebrations, and festivals. On the other hand, significant drinking over time creates dependence, and this dependence is not a temporary problem but rather a physical and mental illness. Addicts die at a much younger age than their counterparts who do not consume a large amount of intoxicating drinks.

Overuse/abuse of alcohol adversely affects the drinker's personality structure. Among other things, alcoholism reduces one's capacity for intimacy, and the divorce rate of couples with an alcoholic partner is much higher than that of any other couples. In many countries, heavy taxes are imposed on alcoholic beverages to reduce alcohol consumption, but an addict's need for a drink is severe, and therefore to reduce consumption, particularly high taxes are necessary. As consumption decreases, the death rate from car accidents caused by drunk driving also decreases, as does the death rate from falls, suicide, and cirrhosis of the liver.

Reducing excessive consumption of alcohol is also somewhat successful due to the activity of voluntary organizations, not only due to taxation. For example, such organizations are working to raise the minimum age for drinking to twenty-one and also to set a lower threshold for blood alcohol level, which is used as an indicator for determining intoxication. The US and other countries also encourage the establishment of random roadblocks where breath tests are conducted. These actions have been successful in influencing legislation, and in recent decades the per capita death rate due to drunken driving has dropped. Advertising campaigns have aided as well: "If you drink, don't drive." These ads emphasize that road accidents harm not only the drunken drivers but also innocent victims.[2]

---

2   See for example https://www.niaaa.nih.gov/publications

Chapter Five

THE MAIN TYPES OF ALCOHOLIC BEVERAGES

1. Whiskey: Water of Life

The previous chapter covered rum—an alcoholic beverage made from sugarcane. There are other types of liquor that are worth mentioning, and the most important one is whiskey. The word "whiskey" is short for the Celtic word *uisge beatha,* which means "water of life." To the distillation processes mentioned in the previous chapter we must add the contribution of Ramon Llull (1232–1315), a writer, scientist, mystic, philosopher, and Christian missionary from the Balearic Islands. In his book, which was copied and distributed in Europe, Llull recommended distilling barley or wheat in copper boilers called stills. These stills have a wide bottom to absorb heat easily and a narrow upper neck. When the bottom of the device is heated, the alcohol vapor is collected into a tube connected to the top of the still and routed to another container (the target container). Alcohol distilled in this way usually has a concentration of 40 to 50 percent, but it is also possible to get a higher one. The alcoholic liquid is stored in large barrels called casks, and its flavor improves over time.

Monasteries in Ireland and Scotland, and later private producers, began to produce for local trade the beverage, which became known as "whiskey." The manufacturers joined guilds of physicians and pharmacists in Scotland, since the drink was still classified as a "medication," but it is known that in 1405 the beverage known as aqua vitae—the water of life—was also sold in Ireland and Scotland for nonmedical purposes. King James IV of Scotland (1473–1513) loved the drink and licensed its production to several local monasteries and guilds, most notably Dundee. King Henry VIII of England (1491–1547) waged war against Catholic Scotland, and closed and destroyed Catholic monasteries in England and Scotland. The dismissed monks who thus lost their profession (as well as their livelihood) exploited the knowledge they had accumulated in the monasteries and became private producers of whiskey. They distributed production methods and the resulting products among the population of Scotland, which already included quite a few experienced "drinkers." This is the basis for the many Scottish distilleries, some of which exist to this day. A similar development occurred in Ireland, and the well-known Bushmills distillery in Northern Ireland received a license to produce whiskey in 1608. Bushmills is the oldest distillery that continues to operate today.

In 1707, when Scotland became part of the United Kingdom, the British government began to raise taxes on whiskey and other alcoholic beverages. The tax levied in 1725 was so high that official production was cut off and tax revenues fell. At the same time, informal production developed (mainly by families), and their products were hidden, among other places, in church shrines and in coffins. Historical studies indicate that in the eighteenth century, at least half of whiskey production was unofficial. Distillation was carried out at night, when the darkness hid the columns of smoke. This is why the distilled drink was called "moonshine." It was only in 1823 that the British government came to an agreement and reduced the tax. Since then production has become legitimate, and Scotch whiskey has become an important export product that is sold worldwide.

The whiskey industry flourished in the mid-nineteenth century. There were two types of whiskey in Scotland then (as today). One is made from barley and is called malt whiskey, and the other is a blended whiskey. Malt whiskey is made only from quality barley. The dry barley is soaked in water; then the grains are spread out to dry on a stone or concrete floor. The seeds and sprouts dry over the course of five days. Further drying is done on a pierced iron floor heated by coal and peat soil, which is the source of the drink's smoky aroma. The smoked barley is then ground, hot water is added and stirred, and after filtering, the fermented fluid remains. Yeast is added to further ferment the liquid. At the end of the fermentation, a double distillation is performed, and the alcoholic liquid is transferred to oak barrels, where it will be stored for three to ten years. The time it is aged in the barrels adds aroma and an ivory-yellow color. At the end of the process, the beverage is diluted with spring water to a 42 percent alcohol level.

The first blending of whiskey was done in 1853. Blending is a combination of several whiskeys, which creates a whiskey with a lighter flavor. Among the first to manufacture blended whiskey was John Walker, a small manufacturer from Kilmarnock. His blended whiskey, "Johnny Walker," is sold to this day. Blended whiskey is close to 50 percent pure malt whiskey, and the rest consists of whiskeys made from different types of grain. Every whiskey company has a "senior blender" whose job it is to maintain a uniform taste. After blending, the whiskey is transferred to large barrels for a period of six to twelve months to allow the ingredients to blend well. When a number of years of aging is recorded on a bottle of blended whiskey, this indicates the aging of the youngest whiskey in the mixture.

There are other types of whiskey in addition to Scotch whiskey. American whiskey was produced in the eastern United States at the beginning of the eighteenth century. The land in New England was suitable for growing rye and corn, so these grains were used to make whiskey, which tasted differently from that produced from barley. In the American Midwest, bourbon whiskey, distilled primarily from corn and aged in oak barrels for at least four years, was already being produced in the nineteenth century. There is also Canadian whiskey, made from a mixture of grains that includes barley, similar to that in Scotland. In 1890, under pressure by domestic whiskey producers, a law was passed in the United States requiring the name of the country of production to be marked on the bottle label. It turned out that the "Made in Canada" label actually increased the sales of Canadian whiskey, which competed effectively with New England's local product.

2. Cognac: Revealer of Secrets

Cognac as we know it has its roots in the sixteenth century, when Dutch merchants came to the coastal French provinces to buy salt, wood, and wine. The journey from the north of France to the Netherlands was not beneficial for the wine: it was transported in small ships over a ten-day passage, and some of it arrived sour. Over time it turned out that distilled wine, with high alcohol content, was better preserved and saved storage space. Hence in Northern France they began to produce a wine drink called *brandewijn* ("burnt wine"), the source of the name brandy. Brandy is produced all over the world, but only the brandy produced in the vicinity of the city Cognac may be called cognac. According to documents from the sixteenth century, the inhabitants of the region developed a special production process and were strict about the type of wood from which the aging barrels were made. Within a short time, their production secrets and principles were discovered, but it was almost impossible to reproduce the special taste in other regions or in other countries.

France is a centralized country, having legal requirements that define which drink may be known by which name. A government bureau called BNIC—Bureau National Interprofessionnel du Cognac—defines and enforces precise standards for the types of cognac. The bureau determines the type of grapes, the type of distillation, and the duration of the aging in barrels. The distillation process begins with white grape juice and yeast fermentation to 8 percent alcohol. The distillation itself is done in copper boilers called *alambic charentais*. This is a double distillation, at the end of which a clear liquid stored in French oak barrels is obtained. The cognac is classified into three grades, according to the duration of its aging in barrels:

1. A beverage that has aged in barrels for at least thirty months (two and a half years) is known as VS—Very Special.

2. A beverage that has aged in barrels for at least four years is called VSOP—Very Special Old Pale.

3. A beverage that has aged in barrels for at least six years is called XO—Extra Old.

The clear liquid obtained at the end of the double distillation is 70 percent strength alcohol, but during the aging in barrels, the alcohol content drops to 40 percent due to evaporation. After aging in barrels, the cognac is bottled and sent to sales points.

The world's best-selling cognac is produced mainly by the giant companies, and the most widely sold types are:

Hennessy, owned by LVMH, founded in 1765.

Martell, owned by Pernod Ricard, founded in 1715.

Rémy Martin, owned by Rémy Cointreau, founded in 1724.

Initially there were many manufacturers of cognac, but a long process of splits and mergers reduced their number. The industry expanded in 1795 when Marta Martell wed Baron Jean-Baptiste Antoine Otard, and together they formed the Otard brand. In 1819, a new company was founded by Alexandre Bisquit. It is also important to mention Felix Courvoisier, who joined the inner circle of manufacturers in 1835. The major manufacturers have also contributed innovations: in 1865, Hennessy began using stars to denote quality and in 1876 began to brand the shape of his bottles. In the twentieth century, the successful industry attracted giant companies that acquired the cognac manufacturers and began to market extensively throughout the world.

3. Gin: The Persistence of Memory

The invention of gin in the mid-seventeenth century is attributed to Francis Sylvius (1581–1649), a professor of medicine at the University of Leiden in the Netherlands. Sylvius studied the medicinal effects of alcohol mixed with medications. In one experiment he added juniper oil (an extract of the juniper berry), a diuretic used as a medicine for kidney problems, to the alcohol. The mixture was called "Hannibur." The alcohol, which was the main ingredient in the mixture, was produced from grains. The cheap grain alcohol, through the use of juniper, gained a medicinal value and, for many, a good taste.

The rapprochement between England and the Netherlands at the end of the seventeenth century and the hostility between England and Louis XIV's France caused a dramatic change in the English beverage market. The English imposed restrictions on imports from France, and as a result almost all imports of French brandy to England stopped. At the same time, imports from the Netherlands grew significantly, and gin imported from the Netherlands was very successful. Along with imports, the production of gin in England itself also increased. In the last quarter of the seventeenth century, the import of gin to England doubled, and the increased consumption of alcohol at the beginning of the eighteenth century was called "gin mania."

The high consumption of gin caused a problem of drunkenness and sparked public debate about drinking liquor. On the one hand, there were people like the writer Daniel Defoe (1660–1731) who supported the consumption of gin mainly because the local brewers provided employment for many and the farmers who produced the grain for the industry profited well. On the other hand were those who saw the consequences of excessive drinking, such as the painter William Hogarth (1697–1764) who expressed in his paintings the negative side of drunkenness. Increasing the tax on gin did not help to reduce its use, because it had close alternatives with other names. One of them was "Parliamentary Brandy." The gin mania did not make Britain a country of drinkers, but it increased the average consumption of alcohol to one gallon a year, turning the evening gin and tonic into an accepted social norm.

It is astonishing that at the beginning of the eighteenth century, Scotch whiskey was virtually unknown in southern England. The reason for this was the high tax levied on the whiskey (see above in the first section of this chapter). Smuggled whiskey did not arrive in London until 1781, and only in 1800 did whiskey become a sought-after drink reflecting social mobility. The increase in alcohol consumption was influenced by three factors: First, the urban population grew significantly, and "social drinking" became an accepted activity in the evening. Second, the anti-drunken movement, backed by the Church, succeeded in reducing drunkenness. Third, the free trade movement acted to reduce tariffs on imports and reduce indirect taxes on domestic production. The government hesitated to lower taxes, because the sales tax and customs duties on alcoholic beverages provided almost 30 percent of the state budget.

4. Vodka (and Jewish Settlement in Eastern Europe)

Vodka is a colorless liquor produced from fermenting and distilling grains or potatoes. It contains water and an alcohol level of usually about 40 percent. Vodka was well known in Eastern Europe some six hundred years ago. The Russian word *vodka* (Водка), meaning "small water," was already documented in the fifteenth century. Like other alcoholic beverages, the first use of vodka was for medicinal purposes, and it was used alongside herbs that were given to patients in need of healing. The distilled liquid was initially murky, but in the early nineteenth century a chemist by the name of Theodor Lubitsch developed a filtering method using charcoal that made the drink clear and colorless. In Poland and Russia, the production of the liquor was a privilege reserved for nobles, monks, and pharmacists. However, over time, the drink became a favorite for all classes of the people.

In Poland and Russia, vodka is produced from many agricultural products: potatoes, corn, barley, and rye. Vodka distillation maintains a uniform level of alcohol. Regular distillation creates a cloudy product, which is filtered by coal and becomes clear. Then the liquid is mixed with water to get the desired strength. Most vodka is produced at a 40 percent alcohol level.

Vodka was not very common in the United States, but the attitude toward it has changed since the 1950s. Vodka has no obvious taste, so it is considered an ideal drink for making cocktails. Cocktails such as the Bloody Mary (a mixture of vodka and tomato juice) and the screwdriver (a mixture of vodka and orange juice) are widely consumed in the United States and around the world.

Vodka is associated with Jewish settlement in Poland and Lithuania. Gershon David Hundert[1] explains the connection between vodka's transformation into an export product that replaced trade in grain and the settlement of Jews in Poland and Lithuania. The transition from grain exports to alcohol export stemmed from grain surplus in the central and eastern sovereignties. The surplus was intended for both export and local use, and this involved extensive production. The conversion of grain to an alcoholic beverage was done to reduce the need for transportation. The complex process, carried out far from the seats of the plantation-owning aristocracy (magnates), required intermediaries, and the Jews were willing to conduct this activity because they knew

---

1   Gershon David Hundert, *A Small Redemption and a Little Honor: Jewish Society in Poland-Lithuania in the Eighteenth Century*, trans. Sufiya Lasman (Jerusalem: The Zalman Shazar Center, 2008).

accounting and were considered fair by the grain owners (and they did not drink themselves). The magnates invited the Jews to work for them and in return protected them from competition by urban dwellers.

In the seventeenth century, vodka joined beer as a drink suitable for ordinary people, and at the same time it was a profitable beverage for the big manufacturers. Vodka was, of course, a tax target. In the Polish crown estates, the rate of revenue from the sale of vodka increased from 6 percent in 1764 to 40 percent in 1792.

The Jews held the monopoly on rights to produce and sell vodka, and this was their main occupation in the eastern part of the Polish-Lithuanian Commonwealth. Hundert notes that in the eighteenth century, one-third of the Jews living in these areas engaged in activities related to the production, distribution, and sale of alcoholic beverages. The high aristocracy (magnates like Radzivil, Zamoyski, Czartoryski, and Potocki) had great power in Poland, and some of the magnates had private armies. They controlled towns and villages far from their places of residence, and Jews were employed in the business of grain and liquor, including the management of taverns.

5. Other Drinks

Alongside the "top five"—rum, whiskey, cognac, gin, vodka— that take up a large part of the alcoholic beverage market, I'll mention a few more famous drinks here.

Tequila: When the Spanish conquerors arrived in Mexico in the sixteenth century, they found an alcoholic drink popular with the natives that is a kind of beer produced by agave plant fermentation. The Spaniards distilled from the agave plant an alcoholic drink called *mezcal*. A few beverage producers near the city of Tequila were able to produce a clean, light, double-distilled beverage from the mezcal, later named after the city (Tequila). Tequila is made only from the blue agave plant. This is a large plant, a kind of bush with long, pointed leaves, that grows in arid soil. Tequila became very popular in the 1980s, mainly because it serves as a base for the popular cocktail margarita (margaritas are usually made from equal parts of tequila, lime juice, and Cointreau).

Baijiu: The traditional alcoholic drink in China is called *baijiu*. As far as is known, it was the favorite drink of the late Mao Tse-tung and is still popular with the Chinese. Baijiu is made from a combination of sorghum and rice, and for decades it has been the favorite alcoholic beverage of the Communist Party of China. It is featured at official dinners in honor of foreign leaders visiting China. Although the main alcohol in this drink is made from rice, it has a taste that is different from that of the Japanese sake, and also has a sharp smell. It is produced by a government-owned company, Kweichow Moutai, which is traded on the Shanghai Stock Exchange. The company has a higher market value than the large British company Diageo, which owns many brands of popular alcoholic beverages.

Vermouth: Vermouth is a fortified wormwood wine made by the Italians and the French from the end of the eighteenth century, using white wines with spices. The Italian version is a little sweet, while the French version is dry. The wormwood was a major seasoning product of vermouth (the plant itself, as a drink, was a popular remedy for epidemics that struck Europe from time to time). Vermouth consists of a fortified wine with flavorings like quinine, juniper berries, cloves, nutmeg, marjoram, and various fruit peelings. The blend of wine fortified with the flavorings is soaked in barrels for a few months until the flavor is fully absorbed. Then the mixture is again blended with white wines, and a little brandy is added to increase the alcohol level up to 18–20 percent. There is often a distinction between white vermouth, which is transparent and tastes dry, and red vermouth, with added caramel to give it a dark red color and a slightly sweet taste. Vermouth is combined with gin to produce a dry martini.

Ouzo: This Greek drink began to be distilled in 1856. Ouzo is an alcoholic beverage based on grapes with anise flavor (licorice) added. It is customary to add water or ice, and then it changes its color from clear to cloudy white. This is because the dilution of alcohol by water or ice releases small drops of anise emulsion that resemble clouds. In 2006, ouzo was recognized as a Greek product by the European Union. It is usually served with ice in small glasses. It is not customary to use it in cocktails. Similar beverages are raki in Turkey and arak in the Middle East, especially in Lebanon. The anise flavor is also found in other beverages, such as sambuca in Italy and mastika in Bulgaria.

Slivovitz: This is a fruit brandy produced mainly in Central and South-Eastern Europe. Slivovitz is a plum brandy, 40 percent strong, made from damson plums, which are large and sweet. The fruit is harvested only from mature trees older than ten years. The drink itself is a little oily and is aged in wooden barrels that give it a yellowish color. The main manufacturers of the Slivovitz are located in the Czech Republic, Serbia, Slovenia, Romania, Poland, and Hungary. In Hungary, a similar beverage is also produced from apricots (a drink that I particularly admire), called barack pálinka.

6. Liqueurs and Aperitifs

In this section, I note some well-known liqueurs and aperitifs:

Amaretto: This is a sweet, almond-flavored dessert liqueur made in Italy (28 percent alcohol). The original formula for producing it has been known for about five hundred years, but commercial production began in the early twentieth century. In Italy it is also used in cooking, in particular preparing sauces for meat and chicken dishes.

Drinks based on whiskey: Drambuie (40 percent alcohol) is a drink based on Scotch whiskey. Irish Mist (35 percent alcohol) is a mild drink produced from Irish whiskey, honey, and various spices. Irish Cream (17 percent alcohol) is a popular whiskey-flavored liqueur with sweet cream and chocolate, becoming particularly popular in the last quarter of the twentieth century.

Cointreau: This is a 40 percent alcohol fortified liquor, based on cognac and orange extracts. It is reminiscent of other orange-flavored liqueurs, such as Curaco or Triple Sec, but it is the original. Brothers Adolphe and Edouard Cointreau began producing it in 1849, and since 1875 it has been produced in large quantities. Currently, after the distillery merged with the Rémy Martin distillery, thirteen million bottles of Cointreau are marketed every year.

Grand Marnier: This is also an orange liqueur based on cognac, at a strength of 40 percent. The drink was first created in 1880 by Alexandre Marnier. It is used in preparing Crepes Suzette.

Bénédictine: This 40 percent liqueur is considered to be the most ancient and has been mixed since 1510 by monks at St. Benedict's Monastery on the Normandy coast. The dedication on each bottle of this beverage—DOM—is the acronym for the Latin expression *Dei Optimo Maximo* (God the Good and the Great).

The drink includes twenty-seven different kinds of herbs, peels, and plants gathered on the cliffs adjacent to the monastery. The essence is prepared by soaking and dissolving all of the spices in cognac. Production takes three years in successive and complex processes, and then the drink is aged four years in wooden barrels.

Campari: Last (in this list) but not least is Campari. It is a mild alcoholic liqueur used as an aperitif. It contains about 24 percent (average) alcohol and is made with essence of herbs and fruits. It is somewhat bitter in taste and has a deep red color. Because of the taste, it is often served with soda water. Another common way to serve it is with orange juice. Campari was invented in 1860 in northern Italy. Over time, it received name recognition and is now distributed in large quantities (3 million cases) in over one hundred countries.

We close with a few more famous liqueurs: Galliano is an Italian liqueur with 40 percent strength. This is a sweet drink with a vanilla flavor that is golden in color. It is sold in a very thin, long bottle and is usually used in cocktails. Tia Maria is a 32 percent coffee liqueur based on rum, and its flavor is dry (it is less sweet than its competitor Kahlua). Dubonnet is a popular 16 percent sweet French liqueur that has a bittersweet taste. In the United States, a liqueur called Southern Comfort, which is 40 percent strong, is popular. It is produced from mixing bourbon with oranges and peaches, and therefore tastes sweet. Last but not least, Cherry Heering is 25 percent strong. It is a cherry liqueur produced mainly in Denmark. In other countries it is called Cherry Brandy.

Liquor and Literature

Susan Cheever[2] writes that during Prohibition in the United States, when it was forbidden to sell and drink alcohol, people still drank a lot. American literature of the period described the situation, for example, in the writing of writer F. Scott Fitzgerald. His famous book *The Great Gatsby* describes people who drink to excess. During Prohibition, thousands of alcohol consumers were arrested, most of them for offenses related to the Prohibition laws. Between 1921 and 1923, for example, some seven thousand people were arrested for alcohol-related offenses in New York City. Drinking together was common in those years among literary and cultural figures. Susan Cheever mentions that in the first half of the twentieth century, seven American writers won the Nobel Prize for Literature, and five of them were compulsive drinkers: Sinclair Lewis, Eugene O'Neill, William Faulkner, Ernest Hemingway, and John Steinbeck. They even wrote occasionally about the phenomenon of drinking. Writer James Thurber emigrated from New York to France in order to stop drinking but died soon after from overdrinking. In 1950, writer Sinclair Lewis protested his being defined as an "alcoholic" and asked whether his accusers could count five American writers since Edgar Allan Poe (who was also a compulsive drinker) who were not drunks. In this he tried to suggest that drinking helped literary writing. This is of course inaccurate—modern medicine knows that excessive drinking has an adverse effect on memory and cognitive skills, in addition to the known clinical symptoms of drinking.

---

2   Susan Cheever, *Drinking in America: Our Secret History* (New York: Grand Central Publishing, 2015).

Chapter Six
TEA (AND RICE) IN CHINA AND INDIA

1. History

Chinese tradition tells us that Emperor Shennong, who ruled around the years 2737–2697 BCE, discovered tea and introduced it to the Chinese. Emperor Shennong is considered a key inventor of agricultural methods and many other contributions, including the plow and the use of plants for medicinal purposes. Legend has it that during one of his journeys, while he was boiling some water, an unexpected wind blew leaves from a nearby tea bush into the boiling water, and thus tea was discovered. Shennong found tea to have medicinal value and that it caused an alert state and prevented drowsiness. Unfortunately, there are no recorded sources for this myth. The first written information about the tea plant and its uses dates from a much later period—the Han dynasty in the first century CE (or more precisely, 221–225). There are no factual details from this period either, and detailed texts on tea and its uses are known only from the seventh century CE.

Tea is the brewing of dried leaves, buds, and flowers of the *Camellia sinensis*, an evergreen plant that grows in mountainous areas in Western China, east of the Himalaya Mountains. Local residents are known to chew the leaves or combine them with onion juice and ginger for medicinal purposes. Tea was, in essence, chewed long before it became a drink. In fact, we do not know when it became a popular beverage. Some claim that Buddhist monks spread its use in the sixth century CE, and some attribute its dissemination to Taoism, because the founder of the philosophy, Lao Tzu, mentioned tea in his writings.

The use of tea for medicinal purposes has been acknowledged for nearly two thousand years. Researchers believe that it became a drink suitable for home preparation during the fourth century CE, when efforts were directed towards controlled growth of the tea bush, and it became a recognized agricultural crop. Tea was a national drink in China during the Tang dynasty (618–907). During this period, China was the largest and richest country in the world. By the beginning of the eighth century, China had a population of fifty million. Two million people lived in the capital, Chang'an. This was a cultural city, open to external influences arriving via the Silk Road and maritime trade with Japan and Korea. During this period, China exported silk, paper, ceramic products, and tea.

The increase in tea consumption and the ritual of its preparation took place during a period of growth and prosperity in China. It was then the Chinese learned about the benefits of the beverage and especially its contribution in protecting health. To prepare the tea, water was first boiled for a few minutes so that the cholera, dysentery, and typhoid bacteria were destroyed. Literature from the Tang dynasty details the preparation of the tea and notes its benefit of being easily prepared by using dry leaves, which are conveniently transported from place to place. In this, it was preferable to beer, and according to the authors, it was also tastier. In terms of production and transportation, tea also had advantages due to a low ratio of weight to value. The popularity of tea led to taxation, and in 780, a modest tax on tea was imposed (by weight). As time went by, refinement of the taste developed, and tea drinkers learned to distinguish between different types of the plant and even the taste of the water boiled for steeping. Preparation of tea in the home became a ritual, and a social dimension was added to drinking tea. There were "tea parties" for friends and acquaintances, and tea was served by the host in a ceremonial manner. The popularity of tea continued during the Sung dynasty (960–1279) but later diminished during the rule of the Mongol Empire. This explains why Marco Polo (1254–1324), who spent years in the court of Kublai Khan, does not mention a tea-drinking ceremony. When the Mongols were expelled and the Ming dynasty came to power (1368–1644), tea was restored as a ritual drink in the emperor's court, as well as among the general population.

The Japanese knew of tea from as far back as the seventh century CE, but it became popular only in the twelfth century, when Buddhist monks brought the methods of growing and cultivating the plant and the tea ceremonies to Japan. It is told that when the ruler of Japan, Shogun Minamoto Sanetomo (1192–1219), became ill, a Buddhist monk aided his recovery with tea prepared before his eyes. The shogun became an enthusiastic supporter of the drink, and under his influence, the Japanese ceremony of drinking tea became even more ritualized than that of the Chinese. The Japanese grew tea bushes in farmlands as well as next to every home. Two bushes were usually sufficient for a family's needs. Drinking tea in Japan is a very complex aesthetic ritual. Its main stages are the preparation of the leaves, the boiling of the water, and the whisking of the brew. All actions are performed with strict discipline, using special tools for each stage.[1]

---

1   Of the many details that make up the Japanese tea ceremony, I will mention only these: To transfer the boiling water from the kettle to the bowl, bamboo sticks are used to remove any remains of the leaves. A special scoop is used to measure the amount of tea leaves suitable for use, and a square of silk is used to wipe the scoop. All the preparatory stages are done in a predetermined order in the presence of the guests at the ceremony.

2. Tea Comes to Europe

The Europeans arrived in China by sea in the early sixteenth century. China was then a world leader, not only by virtue of its population size but also by cultural and material standards. The Chinese led Europe in several fields, among many other examples in their use of compasses, gunpowder, and paper money, and in their printing. The Portuguese, who in the sixteenth century had trading stations in India and Malacca in the Malay Peninsula, were the first Europeans to receive permission from the Chinese authorities to trade with China. In 1557, they received permission to establish a trade station on the small island of Macau in southern China. The Chinese allowed them to set up only one trading station, so that it would be easy to track the movement of goods for taxation. At the beginning of the seventeenth century, the Chinese had also begun trading with the Dutch through Indonesia.

Tea was noted as a sought-after commodity in China by the middle of the sixteenth century, but the first commercial shipment of tea to Europe was brought to Amsterdam only in 1610. It was green tea, then a novelty in Europe.[2] Via the Netherlands, commercial transports arrived in France in 1630 and England in 1650. Tea had both supporters and opponents, mainly for health reasons. A prominent detractor of tea (as well as coffee and cocoa) at the time was Simon Paulli (1603–1680), personal physician to King Frederick III of Denmark. He claimed that on its way from Asia to Europe, tea absorbs toxins; thus it shortens the life of those who drink it. In contrast, Dutch physician Nicolaus Tulp (1593–1674) was a proponent of drinking tea. There were other tea supporters

---

2   Green tea was the favored tea in China. It should be noted that black tea and green tea are from the same bush. The difference between the two types is related to the process of oxidation of the leaves; the longer the process, the darker the leaves become. Europeans initially believed green tea and black tea were made from two types of plants.

and opponents among European physicians, but most of them wrote without any real knowledge of facts, and therefore their opinions have little significance. As an aside, by this point in time, close relations between doctors and commercial companies had already begun. Some doctors supported tea drinking and were financially rewarded by the Dutch Society for Trade with East India. However, their opinions were not always accepted by the public. On the side of the support for tea, we find sugar producers from the Caribbean Sea who supported tea "for health reasons." Tea was readily accepted by the British aristocracy by the end of the seventeenth century but was not as popular in other countries.

In the year 1699, the volume of tea imports to England was six tons. By 1799, imports had reached eleven thousand tons. During the eighteenth century, the price of tea fell to a twentieth of its price at the turn of the century. These figures, of course, do not include the volume of smuggling, which impelled the government to lower the customs tax in 1784. The tariff reduction miraculously contributed to an improvement in quality, and lowering prices enabled every British citizen to consume tea every day. The "taste revolution" was led by Catherine of Braganza (1638–1705), princess of Portugal, daughter of King João IV of Portugal, who married Charles II of England in 1662. Tea, imported from the Bombay and Malacca trade stations, was already a common drink in Portugal, and because of her childhood custom, the young queen drank tea every day in small cups. English court nobility imitated the queen, and the quantities of imported tea began to rise.

King Charles II became accustomed to drinking tea as well, and the British East India Company provided him with premium tea purchased in Holland from its Dutch competitor. The king granted the East India Company a monopoly to import tea to England. This opened the door to a massive rise in tea consumption and to the political clout of the importer. By 1660, tea was served at meetings of the Board of Directors of the East India Company. In those days, tea was considered a commodity with a high commercial value, as it did not tend to spoil easily and its transportation costs were low.

The East India Company began importing tea from the Dutch trade station in Banten (today a part of Indonesia). The importation of tea was initially a small part of the total imports. The main sales in Europe were of pepper and cheap textiles. Textile manufacturers in England opposed the competition from imports, and therefore the company preferred to concentrate on importing tea. At first it was difficult to penetrate the market, because in 1665 the average price of an ounce of tea was about eight pounds sterling. But in 1700, the price dropped to just four pounds for quality tea, and the simpler varieties were sold for less. The breakthrough came in the early eighteenth century, when the British East India Company was licensed to trade directly with the Chinese. In 1818, tea became China's leading export commodity (until then, silk had been the leading export commodity). By 1721, imports to England had reached five thousand tons of tea per year. The monopoly effect propelled the company into a leading economic force in England, which also translated into political power. English legislation at the beginning of the eighteenth century supported the monopoly and banned competing imports from European countries. Taxation was also lowered in order to encourage increased sales in Britain.[3]

In England, as said, drinking tea was influenced and spread by Queen Catherine, but the trend continued. In 1717, Thomas Twining (1675–1741), a London coffee shop owner, opened a new tea shop. In this shop one could taste the tea and drink it at tables

---

3   In the Far East, the British East India Company held a private army and battled the East India Company of the Netherlands. Several wars such as this led to the defeat of the Dutch company in 1784. A year later the Dutch company went bankrupt, and in 1795 it ceased to exist altogether.

before buying it. At the time, women did not go to cafes in England, but they came willingly to the tea shop to taste the tea the shop staff prepared for them. The staff also recommended how to prepare the tea at home and which tools to use. Many women organized "tea parties," which became a popular and prevalent institution in the United Kingdom.

Another innovation came in 1732 when a "tea garden" named Vauxhall Gardens was founded in London, with a stage for an orchestra, food buffets (mainly bread with butter), and tea stands. Following the success of this institution, several more tea gardens were established in the following years. The unique thing about them was that "proper women" (in the language of the period) could spend time there without risking their good name, and so the tea gardens became a suitable and popular meeting place for young ladies and young gentlemen. Women preferred the tea gardens, as coffee shops generally served only men and often served alcoholic beverages, from which proper women were expected to abstain.[4]

3. Luxury Tax Then and Now

The Industrial Revolution began in the mid-eighteenth century. It began in England's textile industry, bringing technological inventions and new production methods and reorganization of economic activity. Continuing on, the industrial revolution encompassed other industries as well. Part of the new organizational culture included a "tea break," and factory owners allotted

---

4   Even members of the lower classes could enter the tea gardens and sip tea there. Incidentally, household servants were given a special ration of tea and free time to sip it. European visitors who visited England at the end of the eighteenth century described it as a nation of tea consumers.

their employees a daily portion of tea at the factory's expense. Tea, unlike beer, was considered a stimulant, and those who drank tea continued to work alertly even after lunch. In retrospect, it turned out that tea, based on boiled water, also prevented diseases through the simple act of boiling the water, which killed the bacteria. As of 1730, tea reduced the incidence of dysentery in England. Other diseases resulting from imbibing impure water have become less common as well due to drinking tea.

The increased consumption of tea also had accompanying effects. Tea consumers used porcelain to serve and drink their beverage, and the factories of Josiah Wedgwood (1730–1795) produced porcelain on a large scale. Wedgwood was the first to supply porcelain to King George III and his daughter, the Royal Princess Charlotte, and in return, he was given permission to claim that he was an authorized supplier to the royal family. He bought advertising space in the period papers and noted it. Thomas Twining's name also became famous in this way. As mentioned above, the sugar suppliers from the Caribbean islands also enjoyed growth, as sugar was a complementary product to tea.

The British East India Company had a monopoly on wholesale imports of tea into the United Kingdom, and for that reason it had considerable political power. The state coffers also benefited from the trade in tea: in the mid-eighteenth century close to 10 percent of British budget revenues were a result of tea tax. Representatives of the East India Company had access to members of the government and Parliament, and their political influence was indicated on several levels. Here we will suffice with a well-known tax-related episode.

The tax on tea was applied not only to imports to England itself but also to imports to British colonies. The largest colony was then in North America. Its residents were required to pay the tea tax to cover the expenses of the British government in protecting the colony inhabitants from France during the Seven Years' War (1756–1763). The war was fought mainly in Europe but also extended into North America. From the newspapers of the period we know that the settlers in the eastern colonies in America did not like the tea tax (to say the least). There was also rampant smuggling of tea without customs tax, which affected the income of the East India Company and the British government. Under pressure from the company, in 1773 the British enacted the "Tea Act." Although the law reduced the tea tax paid by the colonies from ten pence to three pence per ounce, it granted the British East India Company a monopoly on the direct supply of tea from China to North America (without bringing it first to the United Kingdom).

The law was a serious mistake that led to the American War of Independence. The colonists in America, and especially in New England, were vehemently opposed to the law but could do nothing as they had no representation in the British Parliament. They claimed: "No taxation without representation," and on principle refused to pay the tax on tea. They even bought tea from Holland without tax. They also did not like the monopoly given to the East India Company, which they perceived as having excessive economic power to arbitrarily set prices. The protests did not help, and the law went into effect. Only East India Company ships were allowed to dock in Boston and other coastal cities. On December 16, 1773, colonists disguised as Native tribes boarded the ships at Boston Harbor and threw 342 packages of tea into the sea. The incident is called the "Boston Tea Party." Similar tea parties, although smaller and less famous, also occurred in other ports.

The British government responded harshly: in March 1774, it announced that the Port of Boston would be closed until the settlers compensated the East India Company for the losses. The announcement angered the colonists further and led to the outbreak of the American Revolutionary War in 1775. Barbara Tuchman describes this sequence of events in her book *The March of Folly* (1984) and emphasizes that "the policy of the British government which took into consideration the wishes of a commercial company but not the wishes of the colonists, led to an economic loss to England and further to the loss of their most prosperous colonies."

4. The Political Power of Tea Traders in the Far East

The majority of tea that arrived in Europe in the eighteenth century was imported from China. The Chinese, however, were not interested in European goods in exchange (except for mechanical wall clocks that for some unknown reason were popular with the Chinese at the time), and the East India Company had to pay for the tea in cash (in gold and silver). It was expensive, because the price of currency was high at the time. The company's alternative was to offer the Chinese opium, which was grown in plantations in India. At that time, the East India Company was actively operating in India and had no difficulty in increasing the production of opium. The Chinese government objected to the import of opium, but the British East India Company organized an informal trade and smuggled opium into China through straw companies managed by Chinese seamen.

Customs officials in Canton, then the main port of trade with China, understood very well what was happening but were bribed to cooperate with the straw companies, and the opium import into

China continued to grow. In 1838, the Chinese emperor issued an order to prevent the import of opium and expelled the British and their Chinese partners from Canton. The British government, conveniently forgetting how the War of Independence broke out, acted in favor of the British East India Company and demanded that the Chinese change its ban. The Chinese government refused to do so, and shortly following this crisis the "Opium War" broke out (1839–1842). Britain had definite technological superiority, including military technology, and in the first battle, British warships sank twenty-nine Chinese ships. The Chinese surrendered, and Britain accepted Hong Kong as a colony with free trade rights with China.

Even before the outbreak of the Opium War, the East India Company had begun attempts to grow tea outside of China. As early as 1788, the heads of the East India Company consulted with Sir Joseph Banks (1743–1820), a well-known British botanist, about the optimal climate to grow tea plants. They discovered that tea could also be grown in Bengal, and in 1822, they began to grow tea in India. In 1834, when there were difficulties in importing tea from China, Lord William Cavendish, Chairman of the Board of Directors of the East India Company and Governor of India of the British Government, supported the cultivation of tea in India, and it soon became clear that he was right. The tea that was grown in Assam, India, was of good quality. It also provided work and was cheaper than the Chinese tea because of the shortening of the brokerage chain. British merchants established the Assam Company, and then other companies were established to trade Indian tea. The East India Company was finally closed in 1858 after the Great Indian Rebellion that broke out in 1857, in which Sepoy soldiers who had served in the Bengal Empire of the British East India Company rebelled, but that is a story for another time.

5. The Rise of India

The north-east area of India, often called "Assam," is a vast land surrounded by Bangladesh, Bhutan, and Burma. It is connected to the rest of the country by a narrow strip of about 180 kilometers, often called "Siliguri Corridor." This area starts as a plain and as it goes north reaches the foothill of the eastern Himalayas. The great Brahmaputra River divides Assam to two parts as it runs in a 600-kilometer valley. In 1824, Charles A. Brus received some tea plant seeds in Assam and sent them to Calcutta Botanic Gardens for identification.

The botanic gardens were founded in 1787 by Colonel Robert Kyd, who expanded his own private garden. His idea was to collect rare plants for luxury and for possible use. Kyd tried to improve Indian agriculture with better food crops to experiment and eventually grow spices, tobacco, cotton, sugar, and cinchona (its bark was used to make quinine—the main treatment for malaria at the time). One of the managers of the garden, which was basically an agricultural research center, was Dr. Nathaniel W. Wallich, a surgeon who trained in the Danish academy of surgeons.[5]

Wallich was a diligent and generous plant collector and shared his findings with others. However, in 1825 he made a major mistake. He examined the plant that Brus sent to the botanical garden and decided that it was not *Camellia sinensis*. The authorities in Calcutta failed to acknowledge that tea existed in India.

The governor general of India in 1828–1835 was Lord William Bentinck. His term as governor was marked by social and

---

5   When Wallich arrived in 1807, he became a prisoner of war because Denmark was an ally of France, which was at war with Britain at the time. Eventually, he was released and in 1815 became superintendent of the Calcutta gardens and served for thirty years until 1846.

economic reform but also by a quest to improve Indian agriculture. He also supervised the official Tea Committee, a group of thirteen members that made tea policy. They sent an agent to China to obtain tea seeds for planting on Indian soil, a process that took several years. The committee also explored the possible planting of the local Indian version of the plant. They received a recommendation to start planting tea in Assam because they got reports that the local farmers were already doing it. In 1834, a new set of seeds, leaves, and fruit blossoms was examined, and this time the Tea Committee informed Lord Bentinck that there was tea grown in upper Assam.[6]

In 1834, Wallich supported the local tea trees, and planting began in Assam. Several "gardens" or "plantations" or "estates" were created. Brus operated some of them. The first year was difficult due mainly to shortage of labor. But somehow, Brus produced tea leaves from the local brand in 1838. Some boxes were shipped to Calcutta. They were on their way to England and reached London in January 1839. There were eight lots (chests of tea), and

---

6   Tea comes from the *Camellia sinensis* plant, classified in 1753 by the Swedish professor Carolus Linnaeus. The second word means "from China," and the "Camellia" is in honor of the seventeenth-century Georg Joseph Kamel, who was the first to describe the plant with accurate drawings. There are two varieties recognized by different leaves. A lot of water passed in the Brahmaputra since 1840, and Indian tea output grew in size. Within four decades, by 1888, Britain was importing more tea from India than from China. Today, Assam alone produces around 500 million kilograms of tea every year. During the 150 years since the mid-nineteenth century, the Indians also acquired a taste for tea. In 1950, 80 percent of the production was consumed by Indians, and 20 percent was exported (mainly to England). Today, about 800 million kilograms are produced all around India; 80 percent of this output is consumed in the local market, and 20 percent is exported.

they were auctioned at record prices. The general opinion was that Assam tea is not a curiosity but a superior quality tea. Another shipment arrived in 1840, and Assam tea was pronounced as top-quality product.

6. Tea as a Consumer Good

In terms of consumption and distribution, tea is the second largest drink in the world, following water. The production, heating, and drying processes of the tea leaves have made it possible to transport the tea easily to countries far from the growing regions. In the fourteenth century tea was brought to Turkey via the Silk Road, which in the past was the connecting route between the Chinese Empire and Western Europe. Tea arrived in Europe only in the sixteenth century, when maritime trade routes were opened between Europe and China. Tea brought to Europe by Dutch and English merchants was first regarded as a drink of the upper classes. Only when its price fell did it become accepted in wider circles.

In the 19th century, a number of changes occurred in the consumption of tea. As early as 1826, William Sullivan introduced the compression of tea into individual serving tea bags. The use of tea bags did not catch on in the nineteenth century, but in the twentieth century, they were discovered to be very useful. In the Victorian era, the British practice of "five o'clock tea" developed, which was a social ceremony similar to the tea ceremonies of China and Japan. At the end of the nineteenth century, tea was introduced as a crop in Turkey and Morocco. The increase in the number of countries producing tea, the reduction in the costs of distribution, and aggressive marketing (such as that of Thomas Lipton) have turned tea into a popular product acceptable to all segments of the population in many countries. Toward the end of the nineteenth century, an American merchant, Richard Blechynden, introduced iced tea, which became the most widespread cold drink in the United States.

Iced tea, which is so popular among US residents, is sold in many other countries as well. The iced tea is also produced in different flavors, which are obtained by mixing the tea with fruit flavors, such as peaches and cherries. Iced tea can also be made at home, and in this case the consumer determines the taste of the drink. It is worth mentioning another American invention: instant tea. Instant tea is especially convenient for use in preparing iced tea.

Most of the tea drinkers in the Western world now use tea bags. A standard bag contains 1.5 grams of tea leaves and has an attached piece of string for handling. The advantage of the bag is that the consumer can brew the appropriate strength according to taste, in an individual cup. In Asia, the preference is still the traditional method of brewing the leaves in a pot of hot water. The pot is then used to serve all those present, who drink the same tea at the same temperature and with the same strength.

In the twentieth century, the process of diversifying and expanding tea plantations in the world continued, while tea consumption in the Western world continued to grow. In the last quarter of the twentieth century, there was a conspicuous phenomenon of flavored tea consumption. France and Germany began this trend, and other countries followed suit. The world's leading tea drinkers are the Irish and the English, consuming nearly 3 kilograms of tea per person per year. In addition, Middle Eastern countries, led by Turkey, consume more than 2 kilograms per person per year.

Tea plantations around the world are located in high areas, in the range of eight hundred to two thousand meters above sea level, where precipitation is over 1,500 millimeters per year. The height of tea bushes is less than 2 meters. The higher quality tea is produced from the bud and the two adjacent leaves, which are picked manually. In places where the cost of labor is low, the rest of the leaves are picked by hand, but most of the tea leaves are picked today by a machine. The drying process greatly reduces the volume of leaves: 4 kilograms of fresh tea leaves are reduced by drying to 1 kilogram of tea leaves ready for brewing. Tea tree seedlings are grown today in nurseries, after selecting the seeds, the seedlings are pruned from mature trees. After the seedlings reach a height of about 35 centimeters, they are transplanted on the plantation. A tea bush seedling is ready for its first harvesting after about four years, when it is about 1.2 meters high. The mature bush is evergreen and perennial, and it is possible to harvest its leaves for about forty years.

7. Flavored Tea

Black tea (reddish) is grown mainly in India and Sri Lanka. It is very popular, and it is customary to drink it with sugar. The best-known varieties are Darjeeling tea and Assam tea. Another popular tea is jasmine tea, which is a traditional Chinese tea. There are many types of jasmine tea; some are based on green tea, and some are based on black tea. As mentioned above, black tea is obtained by oxidizing tea leaves: First, the green tea leaves are dried and then placed in a stream of moist air at about twenty-five degrees. This process causes the leaf to change color from green to reddish and later to black. After oxidation, the leaves are dried again in hot air.

In recent decades it has become customary to add different flavors to tea. Most flavored teas are based on botanical ingredients added to black tea, because black tea leaves tend to absorb more flavors. The tea known as Earl Grey has been recognized since the early nineteenth century. It is a regular tea mixed with extract from the peels of bergamot oranges, which grow mainly in Italy. In England, it is customary to add milk to tea, but the overall number of tea drinkers do not. In the Middle East, it is customary to drink tea with mint. In Turkey, many drink tea with peach extract. Tea or herbal infusions can be found in almost any flavor, from berries (blueberries and raspberries) and citrus fruits (orange and lemon) to apple and pineapple flavors. There are also floral infusions (chamomile, chrysanthemums, hibiscus) and roots (ginger, ginseng).

English Tea in Literature

In the English language, afternoon tea has been established as a concept usually called "afternoon tea" or "five o'clock tea." In his book *The Portrait of a Lady*, author Henry James mentions the tradition, which he believed lasted between 5:00 and 8:00 p.m., as a unique time that simulates sitting in heaven. There is a special calm during those hours (not to mention the scones and small sandwiches). Henry James is not the only author to refer affectionately to this institution, which has an added social value alongside the sweet tea diluted with milk. Rudyard Kipling also fondly referred to the social event of the tea ceremony. The tea ceremony is described by the great nineteenth-century English author Charles Dickens. Jane Austen also dipped her books in streams of tea and recipes for preparing it. In

Emma, she emphasizes that tea is preferable to coffee, and a whole page of the book is devoted to the description of tea preparation. But most literary lovers, including myself, think that the best of all descriptions is in Lewis Carroll's book *Alice in Wonderland*. The Mad Hatter's tea party is fondly remembered for the witty exchange between the characters. Taken from the text:

"Take some more tea," the March Hare said to Alice very earnestly.

"I have had nothing yet," Alice replied in an offended tone, "so I cannot take more."

"You mean you can't take less," said the Hatter. "It's very easy to take more than nothing."

Dickens describes tea drinking in his book *Great Expectations*. Pip sits with Estella in the restaurant and is served tea in the shape of withered leaves. He must prepare the tea by adding the hot water to the leaves, and in doing so, he reflects about how to prepare the tea. Pip had been a destitute orphan, and now he was a tea snob committed to the finest tea.

Caffeine

Not everybody knows that tea contains caffeine. Dried tea leaves contain, on average, about 4 percent caffeine. The consumer doesn't eat the leaves, only drinks the liquid that is extracted from them. Here are a few rules:

First, a darker tea contains more caffeine. Second, hotter water extracts more caffeine from the leaves. Third, as the extraction process is longer, more caffeine is extracted from the leaves.

Caffeine content in a regular cup of coffee
Espresso Coffee: 100 mg
Filter Coffee: 70 mg
Boiled Coffee: 60 mg
Instant Coffee: 50 mg

Caffeine content in a regular tea glass
Strong Black Tea: 45 mg
Red Tea: 30 mg
Green Tea: 20 mg

Chapter Seven

COFFEE, WAKEFULNESS AND ENLIGHTENMENT

1. Well Done, Goats

According to a popular myth, the stimulating properties of coffee were discovered by goats. The story, which may be nothing more than a fairy tale, tells of an Ethiopian shepherd who tended a herd of goats in a mountainous region of Ethiopia. He noticed that the goats liked to chew on a brown fruit that grew on low trees in the mountains, and after eating these fruits the goats were particularly alert and active. The shepherd himself ate from the fruit and felt its stimulating effect. He reported his discovery to the imam in his hometown, and the imam found a way to make a hot drink from the dried coffee fruit, after he had crushed it and mixed it with boiling water. The imam used the new drink to keep him alert at night when he attended religious ceremonies.

Another story tells of the discovery of coffee in the deserts of Yemen. A nomad wandering through the Yemenite deserts was on the brink of death from exhaustion when he happened upon a coffee tree. He ate from its fruits, grew stronger, and reached the town of Mocha on the shore of the Red Sea. He told the people of Mocha how he had survived in the desert, and as it is often said, "the rest is history." This case also has no reliable evidence, and it should be noted that coffee trees do not grow in deserts, rather only in places blessed with a great deal of rain.

So what is actually known? The origin of the coffee plant is indeed in Ethiopia, and in the fifteenth century, coffee spread to the mountainous regions of Yemen, where the climate is similar to that of Ethiopia. The references to coffee from this period deal with the medicinal uses of the fruit. Although there is no agreement on the origin of the Arabic name *kahawa*, it is agreed that the Sufi Muslims in Yemen distributed coffee initially. They would drink the invigorating drink before nightly discussions of Islamic law. The Sufi scholar Al-Dhahabi wrote about the stimulating virtues of coffee.

At first, coffee was sold mainly in prepared liquid drink form, and only a few people consumed it at home, partly because the method of preparation was unknown to most. Over time, it became clear that the preparation process was relatively simple: only boiling water was needed, to which the coffee powder was added, produced from roasted coffee beans that had been ground or crushed.

2. Coffee and Islam

Coffee grinders in the cities of the East sold coffee to designated shops in the form of coffee beans or powder. The coffee was placed in a small pot or a pot with a wide base (which allows the water to boil quickly) with a narrow opening to keep the coffee fresh. The basic recipe for making Arab coffee specifies the use of a special pot in which the water is boiled. When the water boiled, the ground coffee was added (a tablespoonful for each cup of water), and then another boil. Next the pot was immediately removed from the fire to prevent it from boiling over. After several boilings, the coffee was poured into small porcelain cups and served to guests.

In the Muslim world of the modern era, there were three common points of sale for this beverage: The **regular stores** selling prepared food in the markets employed couriers who delivered cups of hot coffee to customers, and there were specialty shops selling coffee. In **coffee stores** it was possible to buy ground coffee and also to drink cups of prepared coffee. There were also **coffee shops** where the customers sat and drank coffee prepared there. At first there was religious opposition to coffee. Robert Liberles[1] believes that the initial objection to coffee stemmed from the culture of coffee shops rather than from the product itself. Coffee shops allowed customers to talk about the news of the day; gossip about neighbors; play chess, backgammon, and cards; and be entertained by storytellers, musicians, and singers. The opposition to coffee consumption in the Muslim world coincided with increased public demand.

The first documented objection to coffee is from 1511: an Egyptian religious leader named Khair Beg banned drinking coffee in public, and his decree was approved by the authorities in Cairo. In 1534, there was another attempt to ban the consumption of coffee in public, but the attempt did not succeed and did not close the coffee shops. Some doctors claimed coffee was unhealthy; on the other hand, there were doctors who claimed that coffee was actually good for one's health. In retrospect, it can be said that the doctors who came out against coffee and the clerics who tried to reduce its drinking all failed.

Coffee spread throughout the Ottoman Empire. It seems that pilgrims brought coffee from Yemen to Mecca and Medina, and

---

1   Robert Liberles, *Jews Welcome Coffee: Tradition and Innovation in Early Modern Germany* (Jerusalem: Carmel, 2016).

from there coffee was brought to Cairo, Damascus, Aleppo, and Baghdad. In 1554, coffee arrived in Istanbul, where coffee shops were established, combining drinking with social games, narghile smoking, and musical performances. Coffee replaced alcohol in places of entertainment in the Islamic world, since drinking alcohol is forbidden to Muslims. The coffee shops earned well and paid high taxes to the government. European tourists described the consumption of coffee in Istanbul, and the term "Turkish coffee" took root in the description of Arab coffee.

3. Coffee Reaches Europe: The Tourist Version

In 1974, I attended a conference of the Econometric Association in Budapest and spent three days in Vienna waiting for a visa. One day, I joined a group of tourists and learned about the history of Vienna from a certified guide. As we strolled along the Ring Road (the Ringstraße—a wide boulevard around the center of Vienna), the guide explained that this boulevard was once a wall that protected the city. In 1683, the Turkish army besieged Vienna, which was then a fortified walled city of medium size. Even before the siege, anyone who could (including King Leopold) had fled the city. There was not much food, but the army of the defenders prevented the Turks from climbing the walls. The Turks dug tunnels under the wall to bury explosives and destroy the wall.

While the Turks were digging, a large Polish army led by Jan Sobieski approached the city. On September 8, the Turks detonated the explosives and attacked the city through the ruins of the wall. But just as the Turkish front ranks were about to enter the city, the Poles (who were excellent cavalry) attacked the Turkish rear, causing chaos in the Turkish camp. The Turkish army panicked and retreated, leaving behind food and many valuables. When the

Viennese surveyed the remains of the Turkish camp, they found dozens of sacks of coffee. And thus, coffee came to Vienna. The guide told us that the first coffee shop in Vienna, which was also the first in Europe, used the coffee bags abandoned by the Turkish army.

The friendly tour guide told us that in order to encourage city defenders during the siege, one of Vienna's bakers (named Peter Vander) made buns in the shape of the Turkish half-moon. After the defeat of the Turkish army, the little crescents (called *kipferl*) were served in Vienna along with the morning coffee. About a century later, the Viennese princess Marie Antoinette arrived in Paris to marry the future king Louis XVI of France. She asked the Parisian bakers to prepare cakes for her "like at home." The French bakers used white flour, added yeast and butter to the pastry, and changed its name to *croissant*, which means "crescent moon" in French. Since then, many Europeans have begun their day with a continental breakfast consisting of coffee (stolen from the Turks) and a French pastry (stolen from the Austrians). Our tour guide complained about the ignorance that prevented the French from pointing out that the origin of the excellent French coffee was, in fact, Vienna.

This is the story told to tourists in Vienna, but the written history about the beginnings of coffee in Europe is somewhat different from that of the guide. It is known, for example, that a merchant named Pasqua Rosée opened the first café in London in 1652. This is a logical date, since we know that at the beginning of the seventeenth century there was already a coffee trade in Istanbul and Mocha in Yemen. Venetian merchants were buying coffee from Mocha in 1600 and Dutch merchants in 1616. This is evidenced by written testimony from shipping documents. As early as 1650, a café was established in Oxford, but the coffee itself (in a ground state) was popular in European medical circles even earlier. William Harvey, the physician who discovered the blood circulatory system, bequeathed about 25 kilograms of coffee to a medical college in London when he died in 1657. In the same period, cafés were opening in Paris. In the beginning, people drank black coffee. Later, they began to add milk and then cream. By 1669, in New York, coffee was being served with cinnamon and honey, and a year later, a coffee shop in Boston was opened by Dorothy Johnson. All this occurred before the founding of Kolchinsky's first coffee shop in Vienna in 1685.

In the chapter on beer, I mentioned Martin Luther's attempts to limit the drinking of intoxicating beverages. It seems that his attempts failed because no alternative was offered for alcoholic drinks. But when coffee arrived, so did the alternative, and the cafés became very popular. Fifty years after opening the first coffee shop in London in 1652, the city had nearly two thousand cafés. Paris was also patronizing cafés. The coffee contributed to sobriety in the workplace, and the cafés gave Europeans an alternative for socializing. The coffee not only contributed to sobriety; it was also a stimulant.

4. Who Patronizes Coffee Shops?

As noted above, coffee arrived in Europe from Ottoman Turkey and was initially sold in its liquid form, meaning "prepared coffee." In seventeenth-century Christian Europe, the main cities were filled with pubs or taverns, which sold alcoholic beverages, especially beer. The taverns provided an important service, but they had a bad reputation. In France and Germany, it was an accepted fact that decent women did not go to taverns. Public opinion regarded the taverns as shameless places that encouraged their customers to drink until drunk, and drunks were known to be rude. Besides the taverns, there were beer sellers who kept a barrel of beer in their homes and poured drinks for passersby and neighbors. There were also small wine shops, but their economic weight was not significant.

The large beer houses were meeting places for community members and also filled social and community roles, such as keeping letters, exchanging news and information, and selling books. In most countries, beer houses were required to present a license to serve food and drink, and the license was given in exchange for tax payments to the authorities. The taverns were also used by professional guild members, who would hold regular meetings of their membership (usually monthly). These meetings were held in the mornings, when the taverns were closed to regular visitors.

When coffee arrived in the big cities of Europe, the owners of the beer houses saw it as competition and pressured the local governments to tax coffee shops like taverns. Socially, the new cafés had great success, especially among the upper classes. It was a meeting place for families where even decent women could sit and sip coffee with sugar and talk to each other, without a drunken crowd bothering them. In the middle of the seventeenth century, coffee was expensive, but the wealthy could afford it. They were also the first to prepare coffee in their homes and serve it to guests. The coffee (as opposed to tea) was then served in small porcelain cups, similar to what was customary in the Ottoman Empire.

Coffee quickly became a leading drink in Western Europe, and the coffee shops that sold it to customers enjoyed high profits. The social elite in Germany, France, and England made it a fashionable drink, and well-known figures praised and recommended it. One of the earliest recommendations was from composer

Johann Sebastian Bach (1685–1750). He was known then, as now, as a composer of liturgical melodies related to the needs of religious ceremonies. A rare work that is not of a religious nature is the "Coffee Cantata" that he composed in 1735, which was first performed at the grand Café Zimmermann in Leipzig.[2]

The first coffee shops opened in Paris became the focal point for social gatherings, first for the rich and later for the less wealthy. They were perceived as a positive institution, as coffee was not intoxicating; on the contrary, it was invigorating and considered to be very healthy. The French historian and author Jules Michelet (1798–1874) wrote that the decline in the number of beer houses in the mid-seventeenth century coincided with the rise in the number of cafés, and he opined this was a positive process, because "unlike beer, coffee cleanses fog from the body and strengthens clarity of thought."

As in the Arab region of the Middle East, there were also those in Europe who fought against coffee and tried to prevent the import of coffee beans, and sometimes even to close down the coffee shops. In December 1675, King Charles II of England issued a call to shut down the cafés because "they encourage idleness and the spreading of false rumors about the government." Alongside

---

2   This is a musical piece composed by Johann Sebastian Bach. The lyrics were written by Christian Friedrich Henrici. In the cantata, there is a struggle between a girl named Lieschen who loves coffee and her father who strongly opposes the drink. In the main aria that Lieschen sings, the soprano claims that the sweet taste of the coffee is better than a thousand kisses and is even better than Muscat wine. Her father threatens her with measured punishment if she does not kick the habit. This does not help, and in her final song the girl claims that drinking coffee is a tradition passed from mother to daughter.

these arguments, it is impossible to ignore the possibility that his opposition to coffee stemmed from his fondness for tea brought by his wife, Catherine of Braganza, from Portugal. However, the pressure exerted on him led the king to repeal his closure orders, and in the arguments about coffee's benefits, its medical advantages were emphasized. Over the years it became clear that the advantages of coffee outweighed its disadvantages.

During the eighteenth century, coffee shops in Britain became the nerve center of some of the most prominent businesses, including London's Lloyd's Coffee-house, which gave its name to a giant insurance corporation operating to this day. One can also mention the "Baltick" Coffee House, in which the London Maritime Trading Exchange operated. In the eighteenth century, the interior design of the cafés was adapted for businesses. There were tables assigned to merchants, and later these tables were transformed into booths separated by curtains and even into side rooms. Other coffee shops evolved into art and science centers. London's Wills Coffee House was frequented by writers, including Jonathan Swift, and painters, including William Hogarth. In the 1770s, Pascal's Café in Paris, near Saint-Germain, became a social center. And in the mid-1780s, Francesco Procopio opened a cultural center in Paris called Café Procope, where coffee was served as a trend statement. There were marble tables, mirrors, chandeliers, and waiters in uniform. It was a place of luxury, hosting clients like Voltaire, Rousseau, and d'Alembert.

5. Coffee in Prussia

Frederick II, known as "Frederick the Great," was the Prussian king and elector of Brandenburg in the years 1740–1786. Through numerous wars and aggressive diplomacy, Frederick expanded his domain and made Prussia an important power in Europe. Many books have been written about his policies, personality, and achievements. He was considered an enlightened absolutist king, who appreciated culture and science, led his country to (relative) freedom of religion, played the flute, and wrote extensively about history and politics. In the military arena he won many victories and is considered a great leader. Napoleon visited his grave to pay tribute to him, declaring that his military achievements were particularly impressive and he himself had learned from him. The history of the wars he waged is taught in military academies all over the world. His aggressive diplomacy in the partition of Poland has won praise in the history books. His reforms in internal administration and in the courts have also been written about extensively, usually in a positive light.

We are therefore referring to a victorious king and a master ruler. But even great leaders lose from time to time, and one of the major losses of Frederick the Great was in his fight against coffee. Frederick saw the coffee served in cafés as a replacement for beer, and for reasons of personal taste and economic ideology, he supported beer and opposed coffee. He promoted a mercantilist policy aimed at accumulating foreign exchange reserves (gold). In 1752, he published a political-economic document (*Testament Politique*) in which he presented the prevention of expenditure of money outside of the country as an important political goal. The document details the prohibition on his subjects to take more than 300 thalers with them when they left the country. Frederick strongly supported exports and objected to imports. He set up import alternative industries such as porcelain, and at the same time sought to reduce imports, especially "unnecessary" imports such as coffee.

In his book *Jews Welcome Coffee*,[3] Robert Liberles devoted a considerable place to Frederick II's war on coffee consumption. In the second half of the eighteenth century, coffee consumption increased in Germany. At first it was consumed by the economic elite, but later the practice spread to the less wealthy. There were attempts to regulate the consumption of coffee by limiting the number of coffee shops, but nevertheless its popularity increased. The coffee houses had a dual role: first, they were a place where the beverage was prepared and served; second, they created a new social environment, and women would often visit cafés. In the mid-eighteenth century, the price of coffee fell as Central America became another source of supply, competing with coffee from the Ottoman Empire. The fall in prices made coffee even more popular, and the lower classes joined the coffee celebration.

In the big cities, coffee shops were centers of nightlife, and during the day they aided the exchange of social gossip and the distribution of news and business information. In order to attract customers in the evenings, billiard tables and "green" tables for card games were added to the cafés. The high coffee consumption was of concern to the authorities, and they acted to reduce it by means of legislation. As of the mid-eighteenth century, strict laws were introduced in several German states to limit coffee consumption. Today, we find it difficult to understand the detailed legislation that was adopted: For example, regulations forbidding coffee for day laborers, others permitting coffee to senior military officers, but not to junior officers (certainly not to regular soldiers), and other regulations forbidding the sale of coffee in

---

3   Robert Liberles, *Jews Welcome Coffee: Tradition and Innovation in Early Modern Germany*, trans. Bruria Ben Baruch (Jerusalem: Carmel, 2016).

rural areas. There were also regulations prohibiting the sale of roasted and ground coffee. But the many regulations did not help, and coffee consumption continued to spread.

Liberles notes that Frederick the Great was clearly aligned with the resistance to coffee consumption. He cited the negative (in his opinion) example of Poland, which was weakened by excessive imports of coffee. Prussia tried to limit coffee consumption through high taxes. However, the high tax triggered illegal trade, and smuggled coffee was cheaper because no tax was paid. The government's response to the illegal trade was to send troops of discharged soldiers to sniff out the coffee. The soldiers searched the streets of Berlin, identified businesses by the smell of coffee, and checked whether the roast was made from coffee that had been taxed. According to Ukers's records,[4] there were about four hundred paid "sniffers" in Berlin in 1784.

According to Ukers, Frederick II's explanation for this policy was that the importation of coffee from large countries would cause large amounts of money to be exported out of the country, and it was crucial to prevent this. The alternative recommended by the king was to drink beer. He even claimed that soldiers who drank coffee would not be capable of defeating future enemies. Frederick repeatedly mentioned the advantages of the local beer, which did not require import. He believed that if the coffee supply was limited, people would return to drinking beer. In a royal document from 1781, the king declared that "nearly 700,000 thalers leave our country every year for coffee alone, while the breweries that use the products of our country suffer from a sharp decline in

---

4   William H. Ukers, *All About Coffee* (New York: Tea and Coffee Trade Journal Co., 1922).

sales." In the end, the Prussian battle to restrict coffee and coffee shops completely failed. After the king's death in 1786, most of the regulations were abolished, and the Germans became quintessential coffee drinkers.

6. Coffee and the Jews

When coffee arrived in Europe, it easily found its way into Jewish communities. Traditional Jews, who observe Torah and mitzvot, began to drink it while reciting the blessings for food and drink. Over time the rabbinical establishment also approved drinking coffee. At first, when coffee was consumed mainly in cafés, the Orthodox establishment was forced to deal with the potential entertainment provided by these institutions, which of course did not suit them. Shmuel Feiner[5] mentions the problem at length and notes that coffee itself was not forbidden; on the contrary, drinking coffee in the morning was seen as an aid to early rising, and coffee had no negative effect on daily functioning.

When coffee became popular with Jews, the rabbinic establishment was forced to deal with halachic questions related to its consumption. Rabbinic literature of the eighteenth century documents the halachic questions involved in brewing coffee, drinking it on the Sabbath, koshering it on Passover, adding milk from a nonsupervised source to coffee, or drinking coffee in non-Jewish businesses. Robert Liberles covers this in detail in his book (see above reference). In his opinion, Jews accepted coffee enthusiastically, and the rabbis found ways to permit its consumption, even though they could not rely on earlier rulings and sometimes did

---

5   Shmuel Feiner, *The Origins of Jewish Secularization in Eighteenth-Century Europe* (Jerusalem: The Zalman Shazar Center, 2010).

not know the materials and methods of preparation. Most of them stated that the blessing over coffee before drinking is that for "everything," and it is also explicitly stated that coffee is permissible for drinking on Passover, since it grows on a tree and is not a legume. It was further determined that milk and sugar could be added to the coffee.

Of particular interest is the permission to drink coffee on the Sabbath, on the condition that it was not boiled, but rather hot water was poured over crushed beans. The water for coffee was usually heated on the stove used to heat the house. Non-Jewish servants lit the stove in the morning when the coffee or tea was already in place. It seems that the custom was to drink "mud coffee" as a substitute for a two-stage boiling. The rabbis who supported the consumption of coffee thought that it should not be unnecessarily labor intensive, and certainly not on the Sabbath or holiday.

Although there was hardly any rabbinical objection to drinking coffee, there were arguments (as among Muslims and Christians) against drinking in cafés. In the Jewish public there was a trend of religious permissiveness and contempt for some of the commandments, and the authority of the rabbis was undermined. Drinking coffee in non-Jewish cafés was perceived as contributing to this process of secularization. These restrictions had only partial success, and coffee, like tea before it, was accepted by Jewish society almost without exception.

In conclusion, I will note that much of the coffee sold in the eighteenth century in Germany, France, and Scandinavia was sold by door-to-door peddlers. The peddling was informal commerce and well integrated into the coffee smuggling that stemmed from the heavy taxation and the attempts to evade it. In the eighteenth century, there were also groups of people—like sailors and soldiers—returning from major countries with a supply of coffee, and they or their families went door to door and sold it. In general, coffee smugglers and coffee importers cooperated, and the peddlers helped introduce coffee to more customers, who later bought it through the legitimate market.

7. How Did Coffee Leave Yemen?

By the middle of the eighteenth century, there were already coffee plantations on three continents. According to reports, the spread of coffee in the world began in 1616 when a Dutch captain, Pieter van den Broecke, stole a few seedlings from the Mocha region and planted them in Java (Indonesia). A short while later, the name Java became the coffee's trade name, and alongside the phrase "coffee mocha" was another—"mocha-java coffee." It is further reported that in 1720, a French nobleman by the name of Gabriel de Clieu sent coffee seedlings to America. He published this in a letter with many copies circulated, in which he told about pirates whom he defeated in face-to-face combat. And there is also a story about another Dutchman who brought seedlings to Suriname (Dutch Guiana in South America) in 1714. An additional story gives the honor of spreading coffee in America to a Portuguese officer, who received a bouquet of coffee flowers from which he created seedlings.

None of these stories has any basis in fact, and therefore it can be concluded that no one knows for certain how coffee plants came to America. De Clieu's name is best known, perhaps because his story is particularly striking (by the way, spreading seedlings in different parts of the world was an accepted activity of the European explorers who returned from their travels around the world). To date, it is not known exactly who distributed tomato plants in Western Europe and who was the first to plant corn in Eastern Europe.

As mentioned, it is not clear exactly who distributed coffee saplings around the world. If we look at the story of Gabriel de Clieu's adventures, we know from his text that he brought the seedlings to the island of Martinique, and from there they reached Dutch Guiana. During the eighteenth century, coffee plants also reached other countries. There was exceptional success for coffee growers in Brazil, and there is also a good legend about this. In 1727, there was a border dispute between French Guiana and Dutch Guiana. An attractive Brazilian officer by the name of Francisco de Mello Palheta was sent by his government to mediate between the parties. He was successful with the governors of these colonies, especially so with the wife of the Dutch governor. When he left, he received a huge flowerpot with coffee seeds in it, and so coffee came to Brazil.

Coffee trees were also planted in the gardens of privileged rulers. It is known, for example, that King Louis XV had a special fondness for coffee. He had coffee trees that he had received from the mayor of Amsterdam, and he personally cultivated them, and of course he picked, roasted, and brewed his coffee from beans grown in his garden.

It is hard to find written evidence for the story of the potted plant, but the fact is that coffee was well received in Brazil, and there are written documents of shipments of coffee beans to Lisbon in 1765. In order to develop suitable plantations, it was necessary to clear forests and grow food for workers and slaves who tended the coffee plants. It was not an easy process and lasted for decades. But the result proved that the effort was worth the money, and within some one hundred years, by 1849, Brazilian coffee was a world leader. It was shipped to all the ports of Europe. The main port then was in London, where coffee beans were sold at an auction called "lighted candle." Bids were accepted as long as the candle was lit. The owner of the last offer (which was the highest) received the sacks of coffee that were for sale. In the nineteenth century, an organized market for coffee and sugar was also established in New York, and the price was set daily in the regular trading of commodities.

The coffee that was brought to Brazil quickly acclimated to the highly favorable climate, and coffee empires were soon established in rural areas near Rio de Janeiro and Sao Paulo. In the past, Brazil used a method of shading, meaning coffee trees grew in the shade of other trees that were environmentally friendly. But they later abandoned this method, which caused a reduction in the scale of forests and a decrease in the number of winter birds in Brazil.

By the middle of the nineteenth century, coffee had become a common product and was widely accessible to the public. In particular, the product was well received in the Netherlands, Germany, and the US. During the nineteenth and early twentieth centuries, about eight hundred patents were registered for coffee manufacture in the United States. Most of them made no impact. The leading invention to this day is the Italian coffee press for preparing coffee with steam pressure. In the twenty-first century, steam presses also became accessible in the domestic sector.

8. Types of Coffee

Coffee beans are different in shape and color, and their taste depends on the geographical area and climate conditions in which they were grown. Coffee beans are divided into two main types:

arabica and robusta. **Arabica** coffee is considered to have a delicate taste and moderate bitterness. It grows in high mountains, and the cost of growing it is relatively high. The cost in question depends on the amount of work involved in growing it and the extent of the harvest. **Robusta** coffee has a spicier taste and higher bitterness. It is less expensive because the output of beans that a tree yields is higher.

Until the end of the nineteenth century, the use of arabica coffee was particularly widespread, and then coffee plantations were struck by a disease called CLR—coffee leaf rust—that spread in the plantations and damaged crops. As a result, some manufacturers refrained from growing coffee, but in Indonesia (especially East Java) they switched to growing robusta beans because this species is less vulnerable to CLR. During the twentieth century, intensive research in agricultural improvement helped to overcome CLR and other diseases, or at least to reduce their effects. The choice of coffee today takes into account the output—i.e., the quantity of yield per unit of area—and the ability to resist disease.

Coffee beans when picked are green or reddish and must be roasted. Roasting is done in a dry heat with constant stirring and mixing, to ensure a balanced drying. The length of roasting plays an important role in determining taste. Three categories of roasting are used: light, medium, and dark. In a light roast, you get a delicate taste close to the natural taste of the beans. In a dark roast, the coffee oils rise to the bean skins, and the taste becomes smoky and sharp. It is also possible to create blended coffee. Today, it is also possible to remove the caffeine from the coffee and leave the flavor intact. This is done by using water or solvents (such as ethyl acetate or triglyceride) that absorb the caffeine.

The form of storage also affects the final taste of the coffee. To maintain a delicate taste, heat, light, and salts should be avoided. Therefore, all commercial coffee is kept in vacuum-sealed bags to keep it away from oxygen and keep the beans fresh. At home, it is recommended to keep the ground coffee in a dark, dry space, like the freezer in the refrigerator, and prepare it shortly after opening the sealed bag.

9. How to Prepare Coffee

"Mud" coffee is a common method for making liquid coffee in many countries. Place a large spoon of very finely ground coffee into a cup or mug, pour in (almost) boiling water, and add sugar to taste before stirring. The Jews of Cairo in the sixteenth century were the first to use this method.

Turkish and Arabic coffee. A form of preparation practiced in most Middle Eastern countries. Prepare it in a pot with a long handle or a similar vessel used for slow boiling. Add the finely ground coffee to the water and boil over the flame. When the coffee is close to boiling point, remove the pot from the heat, add sugar to taste, stir, and return it to the flame once or even twice more. In any case, remove the pot from the heat before boiling. Pour the coffee into small cups (*finjan*) of about 50 milliliters. Traditionalists pour the coffee into a decorative serving pitcher before pouring the coffee into the cups. According to Bedouin tradition, coffee beans are crushed with a metal mortar and pestle. In most cases, the coffee is ground with a hand grinder or an electric grinder. Occasionally, ground cardamom is added to the coffee.

Filtered coffee, also known as drip coffee, is the most consumed liquid coffee in the world (except for instant coffee). Water near boiling point passes through ground coffee in a conical filter. The water absorbs the flavors of the coffee. For hundreds of years a bag-like cloth filter was used, in which ground coffee was placed. In 1908, Melita Ganz of Germany invented a paper filter. Coffee prepared in this way is clean from sediments and has a good taste. The company that Melita founded is still active today, and the cheap conical filters it produces for one-time use are very effective in removing grains and coffee residue. There are also metal filters and one-time filters containing a measured coffee serving, sold in small vacuum-packed containers for freshness.

French press is a simple device for producing delicious liquid coffee. The coffee produced is similar to mud coffee in taste but without the grounds. The coffee is made using a device consisting of a glass jar and a lid through which a metal rod connected to a metal sieve passes. A cup of ground coffee is steeped in hot water for a few minutes. The water absorbs the flavors of the coffee. Then the sieve is pressed to the bottom of the jar. After straining, the coffee is clear and free of grounds.

Espresso, meaning "fast" in Italian. The basic idea is to transfer steam vapor through compressed ground coffee. This method produces the finest coffee, because an espresso machine can extract all the flavor from the coffee. In the past, steam production was done by heavy machinery located in restaurants and hotels. In recent decades, home use has also become common, using small, simple machines that mimic the taste of espresso served in restaurants and cafés. There are three main types of espresso machines: machines that use compressed ground coffee, machines that grind the coffee before preparing it, and machines that use canned capsules of ground coffee. The use of ready-made capsules is particularly common in home coffee machines.

Instant coffee is a drink prepared from the brewing of coffee beans that undergoes vacuum freezing or spray drying. At the end of the process, crystals are recovered that can reabsorb fluids. The advantage of instant coffee lies in the speed of its preparation, since instant coffee powder melts quickly in boiling water. Instant coffee was invented at the beginning of the twentieth century and became famous worldwide for the coffee brand "Nescafe," which was introduced in 1938 and has since been in great demand. The instant coffee powder is produced in this manner: Water is poured in the form of steam at two hundred degrees Celsius and at a pressure of twenty bars (to prevent evaporation) through the coffee powder, and then the water is separated from the powder. Then the concentrate is conveyed to a drying evaporation device. Instant freeze-dried coffee is considered to be a higher quality than with high-temperature drying, because the coffee concentrate is less exposed to heat. The caffeine content in instant coffee is lower than that of filter coffee.

Chapter Eight
SOFT DRINKS

1. Sources

In the ancient world, people drank plenty of water, but those who could afford it would drink sweetened water. They would, for example, put two tablespoons of honey in warm water and stir it well. In the Middle East, date juice was used to sweeten water, and in the Far East, sugarcane juice. The water they drank was usually chilled, pumped from streams, tunnels, and springs. For thousands of years people drank sweetened water, sometimes adding grape juice or wine with low alcohol content. When the Germanic tribes invaded Italy in the fifth century, these sweetened drinks, new to them, pleased their palates.

In the beginning of the second millennium CE, and perhaps even earlier, Europeans, inspired by local folk medicine, would drink water to which "health ingredients" were added, called *cordials* or *elixirs*. These health ingredients were flowers and leaves from medicinal herbs, which were supposed to improve physical function and the natural ability to recover from disease. How were they prepared? People would cook a mixture of plants, flowers, and fruit, and then add the concentrated extract, called "life force," to the water. The resulting drink (cordial) was of a medical nature and was usually not drunk every day. Over time, the public was tempted to drink larger quantities of cordial, due to its taste being improved by adding honey or sugar. The extracts were initially sold under medical names, such as rosa solis or rosemary water, and their ability to solve a variety of medical problems, from acute ulcers and heartache to depression, was emphasized.

George Cavendish describes the workers in the private kitchen of Cardinal Wolsey, who for a long time was Lord Chancellor to Henry VIII of England in the 1520s. According to him, the cardinal had about thirty-five kitchen workers (cooks, pantry keepers, bakers, and fire workers) and another eight workers who tended to wine and soft drinks made up of sugared water and extracts. During the Renaissance, the price of sugar dropped because the Portuguese had begun to grow cane sugar in the Canary Islands and later, in the sixteenth century, in Brazil. Thus, even the middle classes of the kingdom could drink sweetened and seasoned water with weekend dinners.

At the beginning of the eighteenth century, a popular cookbook was published in England by Eliza Smith called *The Compleat Housewife: Or Accomplished Gentlewoman's Companion*. The book included a number of recipes for making cordials for treating heart weakness, abdominal pain, and more, and highlighted healthy ingredients, such as lemon and orange juice, as well as herbs, such as rosemary and cinnamon. From then until the end of the nineteenth century, cookbook authors added more recipes for cordials, based on juices and spices.

A second source of soft drinks was fruit juice. In the fifteenth and sixteenth centuries, fruit juice was very expensive, and few could enjoy it. At the wedding feast of Henry VIII and Anne Boleyn, orange juice and lemon juice were served to flavor jugs of water. The price of one lemon was equal to the weekly wage of a simple laborer. The situation did not improve much in the following one hundred years. In 1662, the Earl of Bedford paid a full shilling for one orange and three shillings for a dozen lemons. The king and earl could afford the prices, but most people could not. Over the years, trade between England and the Mediterranean countries (mainly Italy) developed, and the price of oranges dropped. As a result, lemonade and orangeade diluted in water became popular beverages in England and France. In Paris, *limonadiers* sold lemonade from containers carried on their backs. In Italy, with its abundance of oranges and lemons, this trend was more pronounced, and fruit juice mixed with water was popular on the street and in middle class homes. In France, cookbooks included dozens of soft drink recipes, and their home preparation was described in detail.

A third source of soft drinks was the category of "small beer," beer-like beverages but with very low alcohol content. There were fizzy drinks based on honey or various roots, called "root beer." They contained less than 2 percent alcohol and therefore were exempt from the tax on regular beer. The most common drink of this type was ginger beer and was sold in large quantities in northern England.

Alongside the water-diluted juices, the mineral water market also grew. As mentioned, Queen Elizabeth I demanded that she receive a steady supply of mineral water from the Buxton Springs. Since then, sparkling water has been popular with all classes of the population. Mineral water was also sold in taverns and cafés, and Thomas Twining imported them to England from France beginning in 1722. However, due to their high price, consumption was not particularly high.

2. Soda Water

In 1767, an English priest, Joseph Priestley, investigated the production of beer in a brewery. Although his main interest was the fermentation process, he noticed that during fermentation a transparent gas was emitted, and when a lit candle was placed in a cloud of this gas, it would go out. He also noticed that the smoke of the candle blended into the gas cloud and descended from the fermentation tank to the floor. It was clear, therefore, that the emitted gas was heavier than air. When Priestley brought this gas into contact with water, it was absorbed in the liquid and created bubbles. This is how the refreshing beverage called "soda water" was created. Priestley gave lectures on his discovery to the Royal Society in London in 1772. Thanks to his discovery (and the conventional wisdom that soda water had positive medical qualities), Priestley was awarded the Copley Medal—the highest honor the Royal Society could grant.

Priestley himself did not try to profit commercially from his discovery. But chemist Thomas Henry, who owned a pharmacy in Manchester, created carbonated water that was actually artificial mineral water. It was sold to the public as a "medical additive," in bottles with corks like wine. Henry advised his customers to add a syrup of lemon juice and sugar to the sparkling water, creating a new soft drink.

By the end of the eighteenth century, there had been several attempts to sell bottled soda water to the public. The most notable of these was a partnership between Nicholas Paul and Jacob Schweppe in Geneva. Their soda water was recognized by some physicians as a high-quality health additive. In 1800, the partnership was dissolved, and Schweppe set up a bottled soda industry in London. Paul tried to do the same but with little success. In the early years, the refreshing beverage was sold through advertising that emphasized its health benefits, a "spring of health" in the language of the times.

In the United States, too, there was an interest in soda water. Initially, there was an attempt to sell mineral water there as in France, and George Washington, who had a good entrepreneurial sense, believed that water could be bottled in Saratoga Springs and shipped to New York City. However, the cost of transportation at the end of the eighteenth century prevented the commercial exploitation of distant springs. Unlike in England and France, in the United States mineral springs were far from the major population centers of Boston, New York, and Philadelphia, and it was more profitable to produce artificial carbonated water. The first to do so was Benjamin Silliman, a professor of chemistry at Yale University. He traveled to Europe in 1805 to purchase equipment for a lab in the chemistry department of the university and noticed the popularity of Schweppes soda water. On his return to Connecticut he prepared soda water for himself and his friends, and within a short time there was demand based on word of mouth. Silliman opened a shop in New Haven and began to sell soda water to local residents.

Shortly thereafter, Joseph Hawkins of Philadelphia opened a soda water business. He had a tank in his basement and a pipe that carried the soda water to the street. When a tap set up on a sidewalk stall was opened, the bubbling water would pour straight into a glass without a need for bottles. He was granted a patent for this in 1809. After this, for years soda water was sold in drugstores for public enjoyment. Soda water competed well with bottles of mineral water, which since 1826, following the reduction of river transport costs, had been transported from Saratoga to New York City.

Soda water was sold both in Europe and the United States on the recommendation of physicians, and intensive advertising also advised mixing it with lemon syrup. Wine was also poured into soda water. Around 1830, soda water began to be sold with syrup already mixed in. Sellers prepared syrup in various flavors, from fruits, such as pineapple and strawberries, in addition to lemon juice, which was (and still is) the most popular flavor. In the second half of the nineteenth century, it was customary to cool the delicious liquid in blocks of ice surrounding the soda containers. During this period, industrial equipment was also developed to produce and bottle soda water.

At the beginning of the nineteenth century, in English-speaking countries there was a competition between bottled mineral water, which often had air bubbles, and industrial soda water. Soda water had bubbles and was sold either from taps in food establishments and stalls or in bottles. The next step up was carbonated lemonade or orangeade, which was actually soda water plus sweet syrup. There was intense competition in the industry, and in the 1840s there were more than fifty manufacturers of soft drinks in London, offering various flavors of carbonated beverages to the public. Even mineral water without flavors sold well. It is surprising that the largest manufacturer of soda water, Schweppes, did not produce flavored soda water. Schweppes's leap into a leading position in the industry took place in 1851 at the Great Exhibition in London. The company received an exclusive franchise to sell soda water at the exhibition and sold more than a million bottles. By the end of the century there were new developments in the bottles and bottle caps of soda water. In the early nineteenth century, soda water was marketed in bottles that were sealed by a cork with a metal wire, similar to bottles of Champagne, but by the end of the century the crown cap was used to seal soft drink bottles, and it is used to this day.

The economic success of soft drinks depended on the cheap supply of sugar, and drinking soft drinks did indeed affect sugar consumption among the population. The annual consumption of sugar in England in 1850 was 11 kilograms per person, and by 1900 this consumption had risen to 30 kilograms per person. At the beginning of the twentieth century, consumers in the United Kingdom and the United States could choose from a range of soft drinks sold at a reasonable price. In Europe, the consumption of carbonated beverages was lower than in the United States, as consumers in France, England, and Italy often drank sparkling wine, which had an excellent taste and a low concentration of alcohol.

3. The Birth of a New Beverage

Every discussion of soft drinks necessarily leads to the most important soft drink today: Coca-Cola. In the second half of the nineteenth century there was soda water, regular and sweet, a routine drink that was very successful both in England and in the United States. It was mainly sold in drugstores from taps called soda fountains. The soda containers were made of metal, and the metal was cooled by ice. The seller would pour syrup in a glass and fill it with soda water. The soda was standard, but the syrup was different from one place to another; often a syrup was prepared on site by the drugstore owner from fruit extract and spices. In the last quarter of the century, inventors such as James Tufts of Boston and John Matthews of New York developed machines for producing and filling soda bottles. The bottled beverage contained the appropriate syrup. Large-scale production reduced costs, and even the less wealthy consumed the carbonated drink with or without syrup.

Pharmacists and chemists produced syrup in various flavors, labeled with protected commercial names; these drinks were called patent drinks, and their medicinal properties were emphasized. Examples of this kind of beverage are Hires Root Beer, a drink documented in 1876 as "intended for weaning" from alcohol, and a cherry soda by Dr. Pepper—a drink first documented in 1885 and sold to this day. There were many drinks of this kind, designed to benefit the health of users at a price lower than the price of medicines, and to serve as a substitute for beer. Patent sodas were advertised as beneficial for all types of ailments: some to prevent rheumatism, others to improve liver function (according to the messages in the ads), and all were said to reduce blood pressure, prevent muscle contractions, and improve one's overall feeling. All this is documented in the ads that appeared in the period's newspapers. At the end of the nineteenth century it was not customary to do a market survey, so we are not able to determine whether these drinks, sometimes called "soda pop," actually accomplished the promised medical functions.

Pharmacist John Pemberton of Atlanta also tried to make his own special syrup. He used the formula of a French drink from 1868 called Vin Mariani, which was made up of wine and the essence of coca leaves, which sold well in Europe. This beverage was introduced in advertisements in the United States as recommended by Queen Victoria (no less) and by three popes. Coca leaves (from which cocaine was produced) were known in Europe through chemical knowledge gathered since 1855. Their stimulating properties were known to the physicians of the period (Sigmund Freud also tried them and described them as a magical substance). Pemberton, who followed the medical press, produced a drink in 1885 called French Wine Cola. This was basically wine fortified with cocaine extract. The original French drink was popular in Europe and the United States, mainly because of the cocaine component, made from soaking the coca leaves in wine for six months. To his version of the drink Pemberton added an extract of the kola nut, which had a similar stimulating effect due to its 2 percent caffeine content. These nuts were used widely in West Africa, where they were believed to prevent malaria infection (with no scientific evidence, of course).

In 1886, it was decided in Atlanta and its environs to prohibit the sale of alcoholic drinks of any kind for two years, in order to reduce the problem of drunkenness. Public sentiment encouraged abstinence. A movement called the Temperance Movement, which held political power in the Midwest and South, created "dry areas" in many states even before the sweeping ban on alcohol sales throughout the United States. Pemberton decided to create a temperance drink to meet the spirit of the times, so he produced a beverage that replaced the wine with caramelized sugar water. He wanted his syrup to be sold in all the soda fountains in Atlanta. In May of 1886, Pemberton introduced the new drink and, on the advice of his assistant Frank Robinson, called it "Coca-Cola" after the two main ingredients in the syrup.

Coca-Cola's first ad was published in the *Atlanta Journal* on May 29, 1886, as follows:

> *Coca-Cola—Delicious! Refreshing! Exhilarating! Invigorating!*
>
> *The new and popular soda fountain drink containing the properties of the wonderful Coca plant and the famous Cola nut.*

The new drink was launched shortly before Prohibition was introduced in Atlanta, and since alcohol was not included, it was acceptable for sale in drugstores. It was a stimulant drink having all the healing properties of patent drinks. Pemberton's assistant, Robinson, distributed vouchers that granted their holders drinks free of charge, hoping that the drink would appeal to them and they would buy it again at a modest price of five cents a glass. The advertising campaign succeeded.

John Pemberton issued shares of his company owning the formula to several partners, who in turn sold them to others. When Pemberton died of cancer in 1888, the company was taken over by Asa Candler, the owner of a competing pharmacy that produced the patented drink.

4. The Taste of Life: Coca-Cola Everywhere

Coca-Cola entered the soft drinks market at a good time: the 1880s and 1890s were years of accelerated growth in the United States, years later referred to as the "Gilded Age." During this period, railway lines were laid down throughout the country, and an industry developed that hired many immigrants from Europe. When Asa Candler ran Coca-Cola, the syrup was sold to drugstores and the beverage was poured with soda water at a ratio of 17 percent syrup and 83 percent cold soda water. The customer paid for and drank the soda from a glass on the spot. Candler made sure that every drugstore soda fountain in Atlanta had a dedicated Coca-Cola tap. In the United States at the end of the nineteenth century, the local shops that poured soda pop from the tap were also a social gathering place; they were open to men, women, and children sitting at the marble counter or at the tables, chatting with each other while sipping. Drugstores that sold soda pop were established in the early nineteenth century and were unique to the United States.

The syrup that provided the essence for the Coca-Cola drink was sold to drugstores in wooden barrels. Candler's intensive publicity was very effective. Shortly after he acquired the company in 1889, sales to drugstores reached eight thousand liters per year. By 1899, sales had soared to eight *hundred* thousand liters per year, a significant achievement at that time. During the same period, Candler reduced the coca ingredient in the formula without changing the name of the product.

Asa Candler fiercely guarded his production process once he acquired the company. Initially only he and his assistant, Frank Robinson, produced the syrup; then Asa's son joined the druggist's staff. When the company moved to a new building in 1898, a locked laboratory was installed in the building, and only a few persons were allowed to enter. Imitators, who tried to take advantage of the success of the product, produced similar drinks—such as Basi-Cola, Afri-Cola, Dixie Cola, and more—but none survived.

In 1899, two businessmen, Benjamin Franklin Thomas and Joseph Brown Whitehead, sought a franchise to sell bottled Coca-Cola. Candler was not enthusiastic, but he was persuaded by the promise that bottles would add value to the syrup business sold from soda fountains in drugstores. He signed a contract with them, set the price of the concentrate to $1 per gallon, and authorized them to sell the bottles in most of the United States. Whitehead and Thomas opened one Coca-Cola bottling plant but also began to sell franchises to other businesspeople based on where they lived. In addition to selling the concession, they also took a commission on selling the syrup to franchisees. By 1905, they had coast-to-coast bottlers in the United States, and sales were on the rise. Soon the two partners parted amicably and divided the market between them.

From the beginning of the twentieth century the Coca-Cola business involved two separate business entities: the original company—which earned its money selling the syrup—and the bottlers—who benefited from the sale of drinks ready for the consuming public. The bottlers invested their profits in the business, bought new soda-making equipment, and bought carts and then trucks to distribute the bottles to the points of sale. They paid salaries to thousands of mechanics, accountants, and drivers. The investment required for the bottling plants was quite large, which is probably why Candler had not wanted to deal with it in the first place. However, the bottlers had great success in distribution. Bottles of Coca-Cola appeared at sports competitions (mainly baseball), filled the cooling boxes in grocery stores, and more. In all, at the beginning of the twentieth century there were four hundred franchisees distributing all over the country. In 1928, bottle sales matched soda fountain sales, and in the following decades the gap increased in favor of bottled sales.

In the second decade of the twentieth century, there was a requirement by the Coca-Cola Company to introduce a uniform bottle for the beverage. A competition was held among designers, and the design chosen had a narrow upper line with wide ribs in the middle and a bottom with a narrow waist. The bottle design was patented in 1915 and is still used today.

5. Is Caffeine a Good Thing?

Coca-Cola's main shareholder invested heavily in advertising, and as a result, the beverage became popular. In the early years the advertisements emphasized the medicinal properties of the drink. Among other things, it was described as a headache remedy. After 1895, the health advertisement disappeared, and emphasis was placed on a "refreshing and thirst-quenching drink." The change came just in time, since in 1898 a tax was introduced on medications, and Coca-Cola was exempt from the tax as it was determined in litigation that the special drink was not a health drink.

From the beginning of the twentieth century, Coca-Cola had become the leading beverage in the soft drinks category. In 1906, the Pure Food and Drug Act was enacted in the United States, led by a scientist named Harvey Washington Wiley. Wiley investigated Coca-Cola and claimed that the popular caffeinated beverage was being sold to children and that parents were unaware of the harmful effects of caffeine on their children. Wiley raised the issue in court and asked for no less than a ban on the sale of the drink![1]

The prosecution brought dozens of "experts" to court from among fundamentalist Christians who claimed that caffeine caused wild sex and could even cause death. On the other hand, the company produced witnesses with a scientific background, who claimed that caffeine was harmless and offered evidence that years of consuming coffee and tea did not cause medical disasters. The sensational trial lasted a month, and its style preceded the famous "Monkey Trial" of 1925.

In the end, the judge ruled in favor of Coca-Cola. Wiley appealed the ruling, and the matter was settled out of court. The company agreed to reduce the amount of caffeine in the drink and promised not to use photos of children in its campaigns. The

---

1   Harvey Washington Wiley was the chief chemist of the US Department of Agriculture. At the beginning of the twentieth century, the innocent American public often fell victim to charlatans who sold "cure-all" elixirs that were actually quack remedies. These were potions that were sold to prevent infection or cure dangerous diseases, without medical supervision. Wiley wanted to prevent the sale of such "medicines." He enforced the Pure Food and Drug Act enacted in 1906 and in most cases succeeded.

arbitration ruling guided advertising policy until 1986, when it was permitted to direct advertising towards children as well, after it became clear that the amount of caffeine in the drink did not have an adverse effect.

Yet even before that, Coca-Cola had found a way to sell the soda pop to the younger generation. In 1931 the company was assisted by the beloved Santa Claus. The corpulent Saint Nick, dressed in red and white, was a very suitable image for Coca-Cola, whose symbol also contained these two colors. Santa Claus appeared in their holiday ads, holding a bottle of Coca-Cola in his hand. Thus, indirectly, Father Christmas recommended drinking from the same bottle he himself held. The 1930s brought three major marketing challenges to Coca-Cola: first, Prohibition—the ban on alcoholic beverages—ended; second, the economic crisis of the Depression in the United States; and third, rival Pepsi-Cola, which began to reduce Coca-Cola's market share.

At first, it was thought that the success of the drink in the 1920s was due to the fact that it served as a substitute for beer. But when beer returned to the taverns and pubs, this turned out to be inaccurate. Nevertheless, sales fell due to the economic crisis, but then, competitors also suffered from the crisis. On the other hand, competitor Pepsi-Cola displayed impressive competition. The Pepsi-Cola Company was founded in 1894, but in its first years it went through two bankruptcies and had difficulties establishing a stable distribution system. Things began to change in the 1930s when one of Pepsi's shareholders, Charles Guth, was appointed to manage the company. Guth had a chain of soda pop stores in New York, and immediately after acquiring the company, he started selling Pepsi-Cola instead of Coca-Cola. Moreover, he sold at a similar price, five cents per bottle, but in larger bottles, almost double the size of Coca-Cola bottles. The added quantity of the drink did not raise expenses much. A price war began, and Coca-Cola dragged Pepsi-Cola to court on the grounds of impersonation and unfair marketing. The trial lasted several years, and in 1942 the two companies agreed to settle the dispute out of court. The main gist of the agreement was that Pepsi would use a logo that included red, white, and blue colors, unlike Coca-Cola, whose logo included only red and white. Pepsi also promised to avoid drastic price cuts in the future.

6. Globalization in a Bottle

At the beginning of the twentieth century, the United States already had strong economic and political power in the world arena, but the general policy was one of isolation. Throughout the nineteenth century, the policy outlined by President Washington continued and was reiterated by Presidents Jefferson, Madison, and Monroe. In the history books this policy is called the "Monroe Doctrine." In essence, it stated that as long as there was no threat to American interests in America, the United States would not intervene in European politics. But in the First World War, the United States intervened and helped France, Italy, and Britain win a victory over Germany, Austria, and Turkey. Thus, American President Woodrow Wilson had significant input in drafting the peace treaties that followed. In the decades following World War I, the policy of isolation returned, and even the aggressive measures of Germany in the 1930s did not provoke intervention. The change occurred only in December 1941, following the bombing of the US Navy in Pearl Harbor by the Japanese air force.

When the United States entered World War II, there was an overall patriotic mobilization in the country. As part of the general recruitment, Coca-Cola chairman Robert Woodruff announced that every American soldier anywhere in the world could buy a bottle of Coca-Cola for five cents. By 1941, the drink was familiar to every boy and girl in the country, and those joining the army were happy to hear the announcement. Coca-Cola was seen as patriotic, and the letters sent by US soldiers to the company showed great appreciation for its policy. In order to keep their promise, real efforts were needed, and with the help of the government, the company was exempted from the sugar rationing introduced at the beginning of 1942. The reason given was that the bottles of fizzy brown liquid were essential to the war effort. The exemption granted the company a "casual win" (a competitive advantage), as its competitors in the US market did not receive such an exemption. Coca-Cola set up bottle displays in military camps near the front lines, and the mechanics who handled them were exempt from home front service. During the war, company technicians set up and operated more than sixty bottling systems, which served all the soldiers of the American forces.

World War II necessitated that Coca-Cola bottles be manufactured and marketed wherever US soldiers were located, and "surpluses" that the army could not use were marketed to the citizens of the countries hosting the military bases. Coca-Cola arrived not only in London but also in the Solomon Islands and Casablanca. The effect was enormous. According to the letters of thanks sent from the front, the Coca-Cola Company was seen as a major contributor to the war effort, and the brown beverage was perceived as an American product reminding fighting soldiers of home. Not only enlisted soldiers were enthusiastic about the drink, but senior officers such as Generals Douglas MacArthur and Omar Bradley recognized Coca-Cola's support for US soldiers. General

Eisenhower was particularly enthusiastic, and after landing in North Africa, he sent a request for a small bottling plant and received ten production systems, each of which could fill twenty thousand bottles a day.

At the end of the Allied victory over the Axis powers in 1945, the bottling facilities for Coca-Cola remained at the military bases for three years, and in that time many countries became familiar with the sweet taste of the "national drink of the United States." One of the favorite anecdotes from the end of the war is connected to the Soviet Supreme Commander, General Georgi Konstantinovich Zhukov. Zhukov drank Coca-Cola in his meetings with General Eisenhower and liked the drink. He requested that Coca-Cola be made the color of vodka for him. The company willingly obliged. The bottles sent to him had a white cap on which the red star was stamped. When the Cold War broke out, the connection between the Coca-Cola company and the Soviet commander ceased, because the drink was perceived in the Soviet Union as objectionable. I will mention here the land blockade imposed by the Russians on Berlin for about a year in 1948. Connection with the besieged city was carried out with the help of planes that, of course, transported Coca-Cola among other items. Although the Russians did not buy Coca-Cola and banned the beverage trade, many other countries welcomed the new drink. It was perceived as an American symbol, along with such values as freedom, democracy, and capitalism. For the sake of clarity, I will mention that there were exceptions. Coca-Cola was not loved everywhere. In France, for example, there were protests against the introduction of the drink, and the term "Coca-Colonization" became a negative slogan. The Americans were offended by the lack of gratitude of their French allies. But over time the anti-American fervor cooled, and today the drink is also common in France.

7. Coca-Cola in the Middle East

And what about the Middle East? The Middle East market, home to millions of Muslims whose religion prohibits alcohol consumption, seems especially promising for a company that markets a nonalcoholic drink. Already in the 1950s, attempts were made to introduce Coca-Cola, some of which were successful and some less so. The most notable success was in Cyprus. Coca-Cola did not rush into the Israeli market, claiming that it was a small market and its entry would cause the loss of the large Arab market due to the Arab boycott. In the mid-1960s, groups of US Jews began to use the media to pressure Coca-Cola to change its policy of discrimination against Israel. Among other actions, these groups created local boycotting centers (for example, at the Coney Island theme park) for the company's products. The pressure made an impact, and Coca-Cola granted a production and distribution franchise in Israel to the Wertheim family. The Arab League reacted, as expected, with a boycott of the drink, and it could be said that Coca-Cola "traded" a local boycott in its backyard to an external boycott by Arab states in the Middle East. The boycott benefited Pepsi-Cola, which entered the Arab market. Ten years later, in 1980, the Middle East boycott was broken, and the company was permitted to sell Coca-Cola products in Egypt, Lebanon, and Jordan. Later, the huge market of Saudi Arabia opened as well.

In the interest of full disclosure, it must be mentioned that Coca-Cola encountered local competition in the Middle East, as elsewhere. In Saudi Arabia, a new company was formed by the partners who distributed Pepsi-Cola that produces a strong brand called ZamZam Cola, which sells well in Persian Gulf countries and in Iraq. A similar product exists in Iran. In the West Bank (in the Palestinian Authority), a product called Star Cola is being produced and is sold in Jordan and the United Arab Emirates.

8. Advantages of a Conglomeration

An interesting phenomenon, which is also associated with Coca-Cola, is that of the conglomeration—that is, the creation of a giant company that manufactures products from different categories. Coca-Cola, for example, also sells orange juice under the brand Tropicana. And of course, this is not the only one; there are other giant companies that manufacture and distribute soft drinks, along with beer, wine, and milk. Coca-Cola's Israeli franchise also produces milk and dairy products. This issue of utilizing economies of scale and distribution requires a separate discussion.

There is an international recognition of the Coca-Cola brand. All over the world, people know the drink and identify it with the United States. There is no other company whose name and logo are more familiar. Coca-Cola is an international brand with a prominent presence. Carbonated soft drinks now account for nearly 30 percent of all beverages consumed worldwide, and Coca-Cola is the largest supplier of soft drinks. The Coca-Cola drink, which contains a mixture of tartness and sweetness, is the most popular drink in the world. It is sold in every restaurant, in every grocery store, in every snack bar, at every railway station, in every airport, and in every stadium. This is a popular drink that has become a super brand. The marketing power of the company that produced it has raised the drink to the summit, rising above all other soft drinks.

Successful advertising and an excellent distribution system have made a popular drink into a shining symbol of American patriotism. After capturing the market within the United States, the company repeated this achievement all over the world. Coca-Cola today is a 130-year-old giant, distributing fizzy drinks to every corner of the world. The company's commercial empire today is not very similar to the original company founded in 1886. This is a rare case of a business's comprehensive and ongoing success, conducted efficiently and diligently everywhere, every day of the year.

9. What Else Happened in the Twentieth Century?

Let's return to the beginning of the twentieth century. World War I interrupted the increase in the consumption of carbonated drinks, but at the end of the war demand rose again, mainly for simple soda water that could be drunk at home with or without sweet syrup. In the first half of the twentieth century, sales of lemon- and orange-flavored soda (called lemonade and orangeade) increased. Most of the extra sales were due to the purchase of soft drinks during visits to the cinema or the theater, or in dance halls that were fashionable in the 1930s. In many locations in Europe there were kiosks that sold glasses of fizzy drinks from the tap to passersby during the day and to merrymakers in the evenings. World War II halted the increase in sales due to a sugar shortage, and some small manufacturers closed their doors. It has already been mentioned that these were good years for Coca-Cola, whose business flourished and expanded under the auspices of the American army.

After World War II, during a period of full employment and rising personal income in the Western world, sales continued to increase, and soft drinks were advertised on television stations, in a manner similar to beer. It turned out that beer was mostly consumed by men, and women preferred soft drinks. Another phenomenon in the 1960s was the high consumption of orange juice, and in the United States and Britain, orange juice was subsidized and served to students in schools. In the second half of the twentieth century, artificial sweeteners (mainly saccharin) began to be used instead of sugar. Towards the end of the century, the consumption of soft drinks increased considerably. In 1985 soft drinks accounted for 12 percent of total beverages purchased in English-speaking countries, in 1995 consumption rose to 20 percent, and in 2005 it reached 28 percent. The increase was mainly among the younger generation: in 1995, 58 percent of young people drank a soft drink daily. On the other hand, in European countries, especially in Germany, France, and Italy, carbonated drinks were less successful.

Another notable occurrence in recent years is that 75 percent of carbonated drink purchases are in household-sized containers, i.e., bottles and cans that are suitable for preservation and chilling in the household refrigerator. Another example is the proliferation of sodas sold as diet drinks, with Coca-Cola and Pepsi-Cola leading the trend. A parallel phenomenon is the sale of simple (noncarbonated) water in bottles for regular consumption during the day and for drinking during or after personal sports activity.

In recent years, public criticism has been directed at soft drinks because of their high sugar content. A small bottle of Coca-Cola (330 milliliters) contains seven teaspoons of sugar, and other drinks are not far behind. According to nutrition experts, this amount of sugar leads to sugar addiction in the younger generation and later to excessive weight gain.

Coca-Cola's Avid Fans

Coca-Cola, since its inception and especially since the 1920s, has a large audience of fans and addicts. Shortly after Coca-Cola began to be sold, people in the South learned to prepare a cocktail of Coca-Cola and rum. Coca-Cola enthusiasts created assembly models of miniature villages with tiny trucks bearing the company's logo. There were also ways to use the beverage in the kitchen to make barbecue sauces for chicken and pork. Coca-Cola cookies were common at church dinners in the southern United States. Over time, recipes were developed for making chocolate cakes that required a cup or two of the drink. There was also a dish called "Coq au Coke"—which requires chicken, one hundred grams of butter, a little pineapple juice, and a cup of Coca-Cola, cooked in a pot over a charcoal grill or on a gas stove. Southern newspapers also featured salads served with Coca-Cola and cranberry sauce.

Can You Fail Occasionally?

In May of 1985, Coca-Cola announced the invention of a new beverage called New Coke, which would replace the original, familiar drink. The public tasted the improved drink and did not like it (to say the least). Long-time Coca-Cola drinkers were furious: some boycotted the new drink, and some demanded the return of "their old drink." Late night TV show hosts Johnny Carson and David Letterman told jokes about the company and mocked the inventors of the new drink. Thousands of letters of protest poured into the company's headquarters in Atlanta, and local bottlers across the United States were "treated" to angry phone calls opposing the change. Loyal customers hoarded supplies of the old Coca-Cola and boycotted the new one. Sales agents pleaded to return to the old familiar product, and the protests continued to flow in until the company relented. On July 10, 1985, the company's CEO announced that the old Coca-Cola was back. In conclusion, the company tried to sell something its customers did not like and was forced to admit its mistake and return to the familiar, beloved product.

Chapter Nine

MILK (AND HONEY)

1. General Knowledge

Milk is a crucial agricultural product. Dairy farms around the world produce about 750 million tons of milk every year, most of it cows' milk produced by 270 million cows, and some sheep's and goats' milk. India and the United States are the world's largest dairy producers. The World Health Organization recommends breast-feeding infants up to the age of six months and then giving them cows' milk until at least age two. Milk is also consumed as a beverage by some three billion adult consumers. Besides the product itself, milk is also used to make butter, cheese, and yogurt. It is used to supplement drinks, such as cocoa, coffee, and tea, and is also an important ingredient in desserts, such as cakes and ice cream.

Most milk sold is produced by cattle and sheep. It is produced all over the world and consumed as a liquid, sometimes in powder form, and in derivative products such as butter and cheese. In most mammals, breast milk nourishes babies. In the first few days after birth, the mother's milk contains a component called colostrum, which contains antibodies that prevent disease. In many countries, children who have been weaned from breast milk are given cows' or sheep's milk. Milk is a useful food that provides large amounts of protein, vitamins, and minerals. Milk and its products are the primary source of calcium in many people's daily diet. A person needs calcium at all stages of life for bone development and healthy teeth. Avoiding milk consumption at later ages increases the risk of osteoporosis, which causes the bones to become brittle and break easily.

All of our body cells need calcium to function well. When cells do not receive enough calcium from the daily food intake, calcium is taken from the bones. The ability to digest milk after infancy depends on an enzyme called lactase. People who do not produce this enzyme can only drink milk substitutes, usually derived from soy or coconut.

A table of milk producers by type shows the large scale of production, mainly of cows' milk. The public consensus in Europe that milk is a quality food has caused an increase in production since the mid-nineteenth century. England was the first to change production methods. Until the nineteenth century, there were many small farms, in or around the cities, which produced milk for the local residents. From the middle of the nineteenth century, the small farms began to disappear, and large farms were established in their place, far from the cities, and milk was transported to the large population centers by train. This was also the case in other European countries, as well as in the United States. Urban population centers consumed milk, and the agricultural sector provided it.

The means of transport and consumption patterns of milk have undergone many changes over the years. In the past, milk was poured from large metal cans, transported in wagons, straight into the housewives' jugs or cooking pots. Glass bottles to deliver milk to homes existed in New York as early as 1870 but became used on a large scale only after the first quarter of the twentieth century. The first cartons for domestic marketing appeared in the United States as early as 1932, but their widespread use only began fifty years later. Wider distribution of fresh milk was aided by Louis Pasteur's (1822–1895) discovery that it was possible to kill disease-causing bacteria by rapid heating and then rapid cooling of milk (a process known as pasteurization). Commercial facilities for pasteurization were established in Germany as early as 1880, and the use of refrigeration to preserve milk began to be common around the late nineteenth century.

2. Ancient History

Milk was a popular food in antiquity. Inscriptions in stone and papyrus manuscripts depict milking cows in ancient Egypt (c. 2500 BCE). A drawing in one of them shows a tearful cow, apparently sorry for the milk that was taken from the mouth of her calf standing in wait nearby. In ancient Babylon, too, the nutritional value of milk was recognized. Nissen et al.[1] tell of "account books" written in cuneiform script, including a report on the milking process and the collection of milk in pottery vessels. Darby et al.[2] report on milk filtration and the separation of butter and cheese at that time. It is reasonable to assume that the ancient Jews also recognized and appreciated milk as food. Indeed, the words *milk* and *butter* appear often in the Bible—in contrast, the word *cheese* appears only once (Job 10), but it may be mentioned indirectly in the expression "cuts of milk" (II Samuel 17). It should be noted that the Hebrew words for milk, butter, and cheese have similar roots in other Semitic languages.

We don't know exactly when goats, sheep, and cows were domesticated. It appears that occurred in the period preceding

---

1   H. J. Nissen, P. Damero, and R. K. Englund, *Archaic Book Keeping*, trans. P. Larsen (Chicago: Chicago University Press, 1993).

2   W. J. Darby, P. Ghalioungui, and L. Grivetti, *Food: The Gift of Osiris* (London: Academic Press, 1977).

written history. But we do know that sheep and cattle were familiar to Mesopotamian and Egyptian farmers. Our forefathers were shepherds and perhaps cattle herders as well, and milk was considered a valuable source of nutrition. In the Bible, milk symbolizes fertility and wealth. The phrase "a land flowing with milk and honey," used by the spies sent by Moses to explore the land of Canaan, became the accepted description. The verse "You shall make your lips wet with honey, and milk under your tongue" (Song of Songs 4:11) used milk to describe pleasant things. And milk was a measure to describe abundance for the prophet Isaiah, as stated in Isaiah 7:22: "and from the abundance of milk that they give he shall eat butter."

In ancient times, milk was offered to honored guests. When the three angels came to visit Abraham, he offered them refreshments of meat and milk, as it is written (Genesis 18:8): "And he took butter and milk and the beef which he prepared and gave them." This was before the revelation at Sinai, when the prohibition on cooking "a kid in its mother's milk" was not yet commanded. Sisera also received milk instead of water when he came to Yael, the wife of Heber the Kenite (Judges 5:25).

Our forefathers had large herds of sheep. Abraham employed many workers. When he heard that Lot, his nephew, had been taken captive, he took "his household, those born in his house, eighteen and three hundred, and pursued them until Dan." In other words, he had at least 318 workers who cared for his animals. In Genesis 29–30 it is told that Jacob tended the flock of Laban for fourteen years and then made a contract with Laban (his uncle and father-in-law), according to which he would receive as wages "every speckled or spotted sheep, every dark-colored lamb and every spotted or speckled goat." There is a story about cut and peeled branches that created this mutation, but it seems he had genetic knowledge that is unknown today. In any case, his herds grew very large, and later it was written (Genesis 30:43): "And the man grew exceedingly prosperous and came to own large flocks, and female and male servants, and camels and donkeys."

During the Mishnaic and Talmudic periods, there was a great deal of preoccupation with the main source of milk of the period—cattle. Our forefathers engaged in farming and raising cattle, and we find this expressed in laws, rituals, and ceremonies. During this period, people had large herds. Rabbi Eleazar ben Azariah was said to have been wealthy and had herds producing twelve thousand calves each year (Shvi'it 5, Mishnah 1). It should also be mentioned that on the holiday of Shavuot, the festival of the harvest, and of receiving the Torah, "it is customary to eat dairy products."

3. Milk in the Mediterranean Basin

In the Middle Ages, fresh milk was strictly a local product. In other words, dairy farms could be found on the outskirts of the cities and sometimes even in the center. But at the time in the eastern Mediterranean basin there was a trade in cheeses. Lane[3] reports that shipping regulations in Venice in the thirteenth century ordered shipowners to include cheese in the daily rations given to their crews. Much of our knowledge about the customs of the period comes from trade documents and from physicians' records. For example, Dr. Abd al-Latif al-Baghdadi described the details of the daily food of the Egyptian population during the reign of Saladin (twelfth century). He mentions, among other

---

3   F. C. Lane, *Venice and History* (Baltimore: Johns Hopkins University Press, 1966).

things, foods such as fish, bread, and cheese. In northern Egypt, at that time, they raised livestock and made cheeses, but local production did not seem to satisfy demand, and the difference was supplied by imports from Israel, Syria, Sicily, and Crete. The mountainous regions of the Mediterranean islands and Greece were full of pastures that were a natural place to raise herds. Cheese was a major trade item in the eastern Mediterranean, and it stretched as far away as Yemen and India. Even in hot climates, without refrigeration, milk was a source of food. Milk surplus was made into cheese, which was also an important source of food.

The attitude of the Jews to milk and its products is derived from the laws of halacha, which prohibit cooking or eating meat and milk together. Jewish law also contains detailed definitions of animal care, including cattle and sheep. In the Middle Ages, Jews were permitted to trade in dairy products and to keep cows and sheep in cooperation with Muslims.[4] Thus, for example, Kallof ben Zakaria, a merchant from Alexandria, reports to Joseph ben Jacob of Fustat (in a letter from 1030) about the arrival of a small ship laden with cheese from Sicily after a twenty-nine-day voyage at sea. Another example, dated 1050, is a letter addressed to Eli Nahari Ben Nissim of Fustat, who reports on a ship from Sicily

---

4   Many Jewish trade documents from the Levant in the Middle Ages were discovered in the Cairo Genizah (a collection of documents discovered in the room next to a synagogue in Cairo, which were stored in this room to prevent their destruction, and the room's entrance was then plastered over from the outside until 1890, when it was discovered by accident during renovation work). Academic works by Goitein describe the contents of many documents from the Genizah. See S. D. Goitein, *A Mediterranean Society*, vol. 1 (Berekley and Los Angeles: University of California Press, 1967); S. D. Goitein, *Letters of Medieval Jewish Traders* (Princeton: Princeton University Press, 1973).

containing "baskets with cheese." Of particular interest is a letter from late 1130, in which Yosef ben Abraham of Yemen writes to Abraham Yazu of India that he is sending him a basket of seven kosher cheese cuts.

During the Middle Ages, there were close ties between the Jewish communities of Egypt and Crete. A letter from 1484, written by Eli Bar Elyakim of Crete to Moshe Bar Yehuda of Alexandria, mentions the shipment of wine and cheese from Crete to Egypt and describes the strict kashrut observance regarding the cheese. It was necessary to ensure that the cheese was made from milk from cows owned by Jews, and written evidence was required. Because of the halachic requirements for milk and cheese, Jewish involvement in the dairy industry was created. The collection of milk owned by Jews or owned by non-Jews was under supervision, and it was required that the milk be processed only by Jews. The price of cheese in Egypt was determined by a market regulator, who set a price for Muslims and a higher price for Jews to include the cost of kashrut. Despite the differences in price, there were also Muslims who bought "Jewish cheese."

4. Milk in Europe in the Modern Era

During the Middle Ages, milk was not a basic beverage in Europe, so they rarely wrote about it. There was milk in Europe, of course, but it was used mainly for making butter and cheese and not for drinking. Europeans have excelled in outstanding butter and cheese products ever since.

In cows' milk there is an enzyme (euglobulin) that within a short time separates the fat particles from the milk plasma. If we let raw milk sit for a few hours in any container, we find that the fat has concentrated on top. Within one day, most of the fat is separated from the watery liquid, and thus it is easy to make butter. The ancient Greeks and Romans did not consume butter (except for cosmetic uses) but used olive oil. Instead they made hard cheese, which was a source of protein for soldiers on the long marches from one front to another.

When the Romans arrived in Germany in the first century BCE, they noticed that the Germans did not drink much milk, but they ate white cheese similar to today's cottage cheese. Hard cheeses were created in the Middle Ages, mainly in monasteries, north of the Alps, especially with sheep's and goats' milk. Cows' milk was rare in Europe. Reports of butter in Europe, and its uses in cooking, appear in the fourteenth century. At the time, the Continent was divided into two culinary divisions: olive oil was used in the south, and butter was used in the north. In northern Europe, medical texts appeared mentioning butter and claiming it to be good for one's health. Yogurt was also praised, but it was considered a dish for the poor. Incidentally, in the German language, until the nineteenth century, milk and yogurt were described as being eaten. The idea of drinking in the context of milk is hardly mentioned.

Consumption of liquid milk in large quantities began in northern Europe only in the mid-nineteenth century, and the phenomenon is related to the swelling of the urban population. At first, the demand was for butter and cheese, and later (to a lesser extent) for fresh milk. Over the years, milk has been seen as a causal factor of disease, especially typhus and tuberculosis.[5]

---

5   In the eighteenth century, doctors noted that milkmaids did not become
     infected with smallpox. In 1796, physician Edward Jenner developed
     a vaccine for the disease based on this knowledge. It appeared that
     the milder cowpox turned out to be an effective vaccination against
     smallpox.

Only after the pasteurization of milk was invented at the end of the nineteenth century did the quantities of fresh milk consumed in northern Europe double. Pasteur turned milk into a desired beverage, and people began to give it not only to children but also to older patients who had trouble swallowing solid food, and often milk was a staple of semolina. The increase in demand for milk was also the result of social movements opposed to alcohol, recommending milk as a drink that was beneficial even for healthy people.

A particularly important factor in the creation of the modern milk market in Europe was the distribution system. Trains, which began to operate in the nineteenth century, revolutionized England by transporting milk from the manufacturers scattered in different places to the big cities. The St. Thomas Hospital in London ordered milk from distant suppliers as early as 1846. The milk was transported on trains of the Great Western Railway. In the final quarter of the nineteenth century, there was already a modern supply system in England. Fresh milk, collected on farms, was transported by train to the cities and distributed by a "small army" of milk distributors to the door of the customer's home. When I lived in London, a hundred years later, there were still neighborhoods where professional milkmen distributed bottles of milk daily to their customers' doorsteps. At the same time, the distribution system was also improved in the United States. In 1877, a company called the New York Dairy Company (NYDC) used milk bottles invented by Harvey Thatcher, which were sealed with a cardboard (carton) disc.

Three factors—pasteurization, a rapid and efficient distribution system, and refrigeration—contributed to the expansion of the distribution system of fresh milk. At the beginning of the twentieth century, not every city had supermarkets, and milk was usually delivered directly to the customer's home. Today most of the milk undergoes pasteurization and homogenization, and that's how it is sold to customers. Today it's possible to remove basic ingredients from the milk, such as lactose, for those people who are sensitive to it. It is possible to reduce the amount of fat in milk and create "skim milk" (low fat). It is also possible and acceptable to add different flavors to milk, such as vanilla and chocolate. At the end of production, the packed milk is transferred to the stores and sold "off the shelf" in glass bottles, plastic bags, plastic containers, or coated carton containers in a range of volumes.

5. Nathan Strauss

It is worth mentioning here the unique contribution of Nathan Strauss (1848–1931) to the dairy industry in the USA and in Israel. Nathan and his brother Isidor excelled in retail trade in the United States and opened a department store there. In 1874, the brothers became partners in the trading firm R. H. Macy & Co. in New York. In addition to his business, Nathan Strauss was a public activist in New York and was a member of the Public Parks Supervisory Board and the city's health department. In this capacity he was involved in maintaining public health. In the last decade of the nineteenth century, when the nutritional value of pasteurized milk was still controversial, he founded milk pasteurization and distribution stations in New York. In addition, he subsidized a network of shelters, which provided breakfast for five cents, and in the winter of 1914, provided milk and a slice of bread for the price of one cent in the stations he had founded in previous years. His stations provided pasteurized milk for infants and children in thirty-six cities in the United States. By 1920, he had established

WHAT WILL YOU DRINK?

297 such stations, and he was credited with a significant reduction in infant mortality in the United States.

In 1904, Nathan Strauss visited what was then Palestine as part of a journey to the Middle East (his younger brother was at the time US ambassador to Turkey), but only in 1909 did he become genuinely interested in Jewish settlement. Later, Nathan Strauss himself contributed a significant sum to establish a milk treatment and a health center in Jerusalem, which was intended to improve milk quality and to fight malaria.[6]

As noted, the first modern dairy was contributed by Nathan Strauss and established in Jerusalem. However, initially the demand for pasteurized milk was low because of its high price (ten mil more than raw milk), but within a short time, pasteurized milk became the standard. It also tasted better than boiled milk.

6. Government Support for the Dairy Industry

In the 1930s, at the time of the Great Depression, many families could not afford to feed their small children the milk that was important for their health. In an attempt to deal with the crisis, the governments of the United States and Britain initiated a program of "milk for children." It was decided that each child would receive a glass of milk at school, and an information program would be put in place to show youth the importance of milk for their development. The program was successfully implemented, and policymakers in each country were praised. Milk is a health

---

6   Later, Nathan Strauss also funded the establishment of a community
     health center in Tel Aviv. Nathan Strauss has been properly immortalized
     in Israel—in Jerusalem there is a street named after him, and the city of
     Netanya is named after him as well.

drink, and as Winston Churchill ruled at the height of World War II: "There is no finer investment for any community than putting milk into babies." Churchill was not content with words, and the state paid for the cost of milk for the children. The farmers benefited from the increase in demand for milk (and the increase in its price), and the cows cooperated and increased yields despite the difficulties of production, which resulted from a shortage of fodder during World War II.

After the war, and especially in the 1960s, farmer legislators in the United States initiated a program to secure the milk supply by subsidizing every liter of milk (not just milk for children). It began as a modest program and grew rapidly. The price of milk for the consumer was reduced, the cows were given good fodder and their yield increased, and the farmers were also satisfied. But government spending had increased tremendously. In order to ease the state budget, they tried to limit milk production—for example, by determining the number of dairy cows permitted to each farmer. On the face of it, it was a good idea, but it turned out that the cows had increased their yield without increasing their numbers, and there were large surpluses of milk that the government had committed to purchase. The solution was that instead of fresh milk, the governments bought butter, which could keep for a longer time and sold well in the international market. Western European countries sold surplus butter to Soviet Russia at a reduced price. However, the subsidy of milk had led to increased expenses and heavy burdens on the public coffers (in the United States, cattle feed—corn and soybeans—were also subsidized). By the end of the twentieth century, sums had reached billions. Food producers supported a policy favorable to the dairy market, but given the budget situation, it was no longer possible to avoid rethinking.

What does the milk market look like today? Government subsidies are increasing production. The cows have become more efficient; they cooperate and produce more milk. The amount produced has increased, the subsidy has increased, and government spending has increased. To limit the expenditure, leaders have set a method of quotas, which limit the amount of milk produced for which the subsidy will be paid. How is this done in the European Common Market? Market management sets a general production quota and divides it according to a fixed key among the member states, and each country allocates its subsidy quota among dairy farmers. If a country exceeds the quota (produces more milk), the European market fines it. How does the country fund the fine? It fines the farmers for producing "too much milk." In 2009, the common market decided to increase the milk quota by only 1 percent each year, thus eroding the value of the payments if the price level rises by more than 1 percent (the population growth rate is greater than 1 percent).

Reducing quotas is not popular (to say the least) among farmers with dairy farms, and they occasionally demonstrate by blocking roads. But it is worth considering the good of the consumers, who are ultimately forced to pay a higher price for the milk they buy. Moreover, because of the high price, it is difficult to export milk from European market countries to other countries. In practice, we are not talking about exporting fresh milk, but about exporting cheese, and this export is shrinking. Another component of the equation is the import of fodder. Increased production of milk, due to subsidies, forces an increase in the import of fodder to feed dairy cows.

The quota system causes further disparity: Some countries—such as Italy and Austria—can produce milk at a price that is cheaper than the quota allocated by the European market. On the other hand, there are less efficient countries that are struggling to produce more just to take full advantage of the subsidy they receive. The same disparity exists for farmers in each of the common market countries. Efficient farmers avoid limiting production, and less efficient farmers produce more because they have large production quotas. In addition, there is a high administrative cost in registering and allocating the quotas and in monitoring the fines imposed on those who exceed them. As a result, the European market is making efforts to reduce quotas (as are other countries).

As subsidies for agriculture continued to grow, proposals were also made to reduce those subsidies. There were proposals to reduce the price target (the minimum price) that the government would agree to pay farmers raising dairy cows. There were also proposals to change the scope of production quotas. Legislators argued that budgetary funds should be released for other social purposes. On the other hand, supporters of the subsidies felt that cutting subsidies on milk and its producers would cause milk shortages and dairy closures and even the need to import milk from abroad. While the arguments for and against continued in Europe and the United States, the New Zealand government cut the scale of government support at the beginning of the twenty-first century. Surprisingly, there was no shortage. Every citizen in New Zealand can buy milk at will, and not only is there no shortage, but exports of milk powder and other dairy products continue to Japan and China. It turned out that the market forces were operating well without government assistance. The Australian government has taken a similar approach and reduced support for milk producers, and there is no shortage. The experience in

New Zealand and Australia reinforced the arguments of the critics, who have proposed a similar policy in their countries. Indeed, the European market is making renewed efforts to reduce subsidies.

7. Special Milk-Based Beverages

Ayran: a yogurt-based drink with ice water and salt added to it. The drink is popular in Turkey, Azerbaijan, Iran, and Central Asian countries such as Kazakhstan and Kyrgyzstan. In the last decade of the twentieth century, we lived in Turkey every summer and enjoyed this special drink. *Ayran* has been mentioned in writings for a thousand years. In Turkey it is very popular. The current version is made of cows' milk, but there are other variations, such as a drink called *chal* made from camels' milk, and a drink called *kumis* made from fermented horses' milk. Ayran is served in glasses in the modern version or in metal cups in the traditional version.

Kefir: a milk-based beverage supplemented with "kefir grains," which are a combination of probiotic bacteria and yeast. The yeast is grown in milk for one day. The fermentation process reduces the amount of lactose in the drink (and thus is different from yogurt). Kefir is considered a healthy and nutritious drink; it should be drunk immediately after preparation or after brief storage in the refrigerator (only a few days). This is a mildly carbonated drink and a little alcoholic. It originated in the Caucasus and is consumed in large quantities in Russia.

Lassi: a popular traditional drink in the subcontinent of India. It looks like diluted yogurt with sugar, crushed fruit, and spices added. Lassi in the north is usually salty, and in the south, it is a sweeter version containing more crushed fruit. If you dilute lassi with a large amount of water, you get *chaas*, served with salt and cumin seeds.

8. Technical Definitions for Milk Products

Pasteurization (named after Louis Pasteur): a process that kills microorganisms found in milk. Heating the milk enables the destruction of most bacteria without affecting the milk composition and its properties. Pasteurization includes two stages: in the first stage, the milk is heated to a certain temperature and for a period sufficient to destroy the pathogenic bacteria, and in the second stage, the milk is cooled to four degrees Celsius so that the remaining bacteria cannot reproduce again quickly. There are two pasteurization methods: a. Regular pasteurization—lasts thirty minutes at a temperature of sixty-four degrees—and b. Fast pasteurization—lasts two minutes at a temperature of seventy-two degrees. In regular pasteurization 99.9 percent of the harmful bacteria are destroyed. Pasteurization does not change the caloric value of milk and does not affect sugar and most vitamins. Its advantage is that the pasteurized milk can be kept refrigerated for more than a week.

Homogenization: fresh milk that stands for a day or two goes through a process in which the fat separates from the watery part, and the fat globules attach to each other and rise to the top of the container. To prevent this, homogenization is used, which is a process of reducing the size of fat droplets in milk. This is accomplished by compressing the milk through a narrow spout at high velocity under pressure of about 200 atm and at a temperature of sixty–eighty degrees Celsius. The process causes the fat cells to break into tiny balls that do not float above the watery fluid, and the milk consistency remains uniform.

Sterilization: a process that destroys all the bacteria and spores in milk, and therefore sterilized milk may be stored at regular temperatures. Sterilization is done by heating the milk to temperatures above one hundred degrees Celsius in enclosed facilities under pressure. The time required for sterilization depends on the temperature. Milk is usually sterilized at about one hundred and ten degrees for forty-five minutes. Sterilized milk has a different flavor than fresh milk, and its color is slightly different due to the caramelization of protein and sugar. Its texture is a bit creamy, and it is mainly used as an addition to coffee and desserts.

Condensation: condensed milk is made from whole milk with added sugar. The milk is condensed to half of its original volume and it becomes syrupy; then 15 to 18 percent sucrose is added. This product is well preserved and is used in some countries as baby food. It is also added to coffee, tea, cocoa, and sweets.

Evaporation: powdered milk is achieved through the complete evaporation of water in milk. The powder is created in a vacuum at sixty degrees Celsius. The milk is pressure sprayed through narrow spouts. When it resembles mist, it enters a jet of hot air (one hundred and forty degrees), and then the water evaporates and the powder falls into trays where it collects. Another method is to dry the milk on a rotating plate, and through centrifugal force mist drops spray into a jet of hot air. The powderization at sixty degrees Celsius preserves the protein, and the powder that is formed is completely soluble in water. Milk powder contains a lot of air that can damage fat (by oxidation), and therefore it is produced from skim milk.

Chapter Ten

COCOA—
THE DRINK OF NOBILITY

1. From Plantation to Cup

The cocoa drink is produced from cocoa beans, which also produce the solid chocolate that is eaten in various forms. The word *cocoa* comes from Spanish and is derived from the Aztec language. In this chapter, the word *cocoa* refers to the beverage and the word *chocolate* to the solid sweet.

The cocoa tree originates in Mexico and Central America, and also grows in Colombia and Venezuela. In these countries it was known as a fruit tree even before the Spaniards arrived in America at the end of the fifteenth century. It may have been used to produce beverages as early as 1400 BCE. Swedish scholar Carl Linnaeus (1707–1778), who studied the cacao tree from a botanical perspective, mentions that cocoa is called *Theobroma* (food of the Gods) in the Aztec tongue. But despite being called "food," it was used only as the base for a beverage. Cocoa beans were brought to Europe by the Spanish, and the drink became popular on the Continent in the mid-seventeenth century.

The cocoa fruit contains thirty to fifty sweet seeds, or pale brown beans, encased in pulp in a round pod with a tough rind. There are three varieties: Criollo, Trinitario, and Forastero. The most common is Forastero. The tree is not particularly high and grows in humid tropical climates, between twenty degrees north and south of the equator. The fresh fruit has a green color with hues of purple, which becomes yellow or orange when it ripens. The pods grow directly on the tree trunk or on particularly thick branches. The clusters of pods on the tree do not all ripen at the same time, so the harvest lasts all season. Harvesting is done with a curved knife on a long pole. A skilled worker can harvest about six hundred pods a day.

The beans (seeds), with the pulp layer, are removed from the rinds and stacked in small piles, usually on trays, and placed for several days to "sweat," or to ferment in the open air. During fermentation, the pulp that surrounds the beans becomes liquid and drains away, leaving only the beans. A typical pod contains thirty to fifty beans, each weighing about forty grams. A skilled worker separates the beans from about two thousand pods per day. The wet beans are transferred to undergo another fermentation, lasting about a week, then dried for nearly two weeks. Dried beans are delivered in jute bags or in containers suitable for processing in factories. In Central America, the ground beans are also used as a food ingredient, especially in casserole dishes, and are mixed with hot pepper, cinnamon, or vanilla. The main use of cocoa beans is for drinking. The global yield of cocoa beans is close to five million tons (5,100,000 kilograms in 2013). The main countries producing cocoa beans today are the Ivory Coast, Ghana, Indonesia, Nigeria, Cameroon, and Brazil.

Today, cocoa beans are commodities that undergo several stages of processing from the plantation to the end consumer. Their main product is a beverage whose nature we will discuss further. Only in the twentieth century did cocoa beans become a solid food commonly used as the chocolate we are familiar with. In the past, the prices of cocoa beans were very inconsistent, mainly because of fluctuations in supply due to weather and changes in expenses required for tree planting. Changes in taxation policy also affected the price. In recent years, the fluctuations have become more stable.

In the history of cocoa, the period between the eighteenth and nineteenth centuries is particularly interesting. At the beginning of this period, cocoa was grown on small plantations worked by slaves; then as slavery was halted in most countries, production was concentrated on large farms and moved from Central America to African countries. The changes in production did not cause many changes in consumption, but gradually cocoa changed from a product for the wealthy to a cheaper product that even the middle classes could afford. These changes will be the focus of our discussion.

2. Cocoa and Its Substitutes

Cocoa contains theobromine, an alkaloid that stimulates alertness and even creates mild addiction. Theobromine affects the nervous system less than coffee or tea, which contains more caffeine, and like those beverages, it was once regarded as a good substitute for alcohol. Throughout history, cocoa has had health benefits (as with tea and coffee), as it was prepared as a hot drink—typically more hygienic than cold drinks. Drinking hot cocoa was especially suited to the cold countries of northern Europe. Cocoa slowly entered Europe, but by the middle of the nineteenth century it held a prominent place on the list of hot beverages.

When the Spaniards arrived in Central America at the end of the fifteenth century, cocoa seeds were often used as currency; perhaps the saying that in America "money grows on trees" is based on this fact. The main use of cocoa in America during this period was as an unsweetened drink, with pepper powder added. Only later was sugar added to sweeten the drink. In the sixteenth century, the major cocoa consumption was in Latin American countries—Central America, Colombia, and Peru. The cocoa that arrived in Europe was first introduced in Spain and later spread to France. In northern Europe, cocoa faced tough competition from coffee and tea. In the Far East and Ottoman Turkey there was a clear preference for tea. The main consumers of cocoa in India were then Catholic missionaries, rather than members of the local population. In the Middle East the preference has been for coffee since the sixteenth century, as well as in North Africa.

In Catholic Europe, and especially in Spain and Italy, cocoa was a favorite drink among the nobility and the clergy. Cocoa also found its way to England and its colonies, and already in 1712, marketing ads were published for cocoa in Boston. In Virginia they drank cocoa in the French style (that is, with milk and sugar). Recipes brought from Spain, including the recommendation to add egg yolk to cocoa, were rejected in English colonies. Cocoa had devotees such as John Adams and Thomas Jefferson, the second and third presidents of the United States. Jefferson believed that cocoa had more nutritional value than tea and coffee. Historians of Latin America have emphasized that cocoa was a leading beverage in the eighteenth century only in these countries. Most people drank it at least twice a day, and households kept a stone grinder just to grind cocoa beans. In Central America, cocoa was not only a beverage, it was also a food, and it had no competition. In Cuba, for example, cocoa (like coffee) was a beverage for hosting friends at the end of the daily siesta. Incidentally, the cocoa was cheap, and sugar from local farms was even cheaper. In South America, mainly in Venezuela, cocoa was a basic consumer product as early as the seventeenth century.

3. Changes in the Nineteenth Century

It would not be a mistake to say that by the end of the eighteenth century, cocoa was a local beverage, consumed mainly by the poor classes in Central and South America. At the end of the century, cocoa plants were transferred to Southeast Asia (mainly to Indonesia) and to Equatorial Africa, but world consumption did not increase significantly. On the other hand, the South American wars of independence from Spain did not affect the supply of cocoa beans either.

In 1828, Dutchman C. J. van Houten registered a patent for the compression of cocoa butter to form solid lumps. At first this new product was not accepted even in the Netherlands, but after a few years the Dutch began to use the solid chocolate to create their cocoa drink: they would pour very hot milk or water on lumps of the chocolate (not sweetened). The resulting drink was more syrupy than the drink called Dutch cocoa, made from cocoa powder. It became popular later in the nineteenth century.

As cocoa became more widely known and popular, it attracted the attention of the writers of the period. Balzac loved coffee and rejected cocoa, which he believed contributed to the fall of the Spanish Empire. As was customary in literature, he saw no need to explain the connection he perceived between cocoa and politics. Flaubert claimed that cocoa was a morning beverage for the wealthy. Dickens linked the cocoa drink to idle priests and was not impressed. Goethe, on the other hand, liked to drink cocoa and was tired of coffee. Despite the negative publicity from many writers, cocoa consumption in Europe increased. The main reason for this was that in 1824, the British fleet determined that cocoa would be part of sailors' daily diet, while at the same time members of the European abstinence movement recommended the cocoa drink as an alternative to alcohol. In 1880, researchers estimated the number of tea drinkers in the world at 500 million, compared with about 200 million coffee consumers and 50 million cocoa drinkers. In other words, cocoa had captured a legitimate place among hot beverages.

Towards the end of the nineteenth century, France became the largest European importer of cocoa beans, surpassing Spain. The French also began to consume solid chocolate. In France, chocolate also found its way into recipes and cookbooks. And what is good for the French is usually good for others. In Britain, too, cocoa was being sipped in increasing quantities, perhaps because of the advertisements that described the beverage as particularly healthy.

Agatha Christie, in her book *The Mysterious Affair at Styles*, writes of "the lady of the manor who during the First World War economizes by skipping late dinner, but will not give up her nightly cup of cocoa spiked with rum." In the United States, too, consumption increased, and there people even added sweet ice cream to their cocoa with no thought of counting calories. In Germany at the time, it was generally accepted that cocoa was the best drink for manual laborers because it was nutritious and rich in protein and with more fat than tea and coffee.

4. Cocoa Trends

Cocoa as a beverage was discovered by the Spanish when they conquered Central America. They brought it to their country at the beginning of the sixteenth century (but the drink became fashionable in Europe only in the nineteenth century, and even more in the twentieth century). Columbus brought samples of the plant to King Ferdinand, patron of his exploration voyages. Hernán Cortés (1485–1547), the conqueror and governor of Spanish Mexico, brought cocoa beans to Spain along with the Aztec recipe for the production of the drink. The Spanish nobility loved the beverage and consumed it with pleasure, but for a hundred years it was not favored by nobility in other European countries. In the sixteenth century, there was little information about the usefulness of the beans, and therefore little importance was attributed to them. The pirates who worked in the service of Queen Elizabeth of England—Francis Drake (c. 1540–1596) and Martin Frobisher (c. 1535–1594)—used to attack Spanish ships. When Spanish merchant ships were captured on their way from Central America to Spain, the British would throw the sacks full of cocoa beans into the sea, to lessen the load and facilitate the voyage.

Legend has it that the cocoa came to France for political reasons. When the king of France, Henri IV, was assassinated in 1610, the heir to the throne (later Louis XIII) was nine years old. His mother, Marie de' Medici, acted as regent and thought that a political alliance with Spain would strengthen France's standing in Europe. She therefore suggested that her son marry Anne, daughter of Philip III of Spain, and that one of her daughters, the sister of the designated French king, would marry the designated king of Spain, Philip IV. The double marriage was celebrated in 1615. The Spanish king's daughter loved to drink cocoa and brought a large supply to the French court. From her, the noblemen of France learned to drink the dark brown beverage. Louis XIV's wife (from 1660) was also a daughter of the king of Spain, and she too drank sweet cocoa every night.

The historical truth is a bit different. Spanish monks and priests who moved from Spain to France and Germany brought cocoa with them to the different monasteries, and from there, the drink was adopted by the nobility. In addition, in 1613 a book was published in Madrid detailing the drink's preparation and its benefits. The book was also translated into French and English. In any case, the sweet brown drink was well received among the French aristocracy. An interesting description of the drink is found in letters sent by Madame de Sévigné (1626–1696) to her daughter, Madame de Grignan. Among other things, the mother wrote that the nutritious drink enabled her and her friends to fast between breakfast and dinner.[1]

Not only Madame de Sévigné was impressed by cocoa, the Catholic Church also had something to say. Physician Gaspar Caldera claimed that cocoa was similar to food, so it should be avoided during the fast days of Lent. Cardinal Barbaccio, on the other hand, claimed that the cocoa was a drink like any other beverage, and that it could be drunk during the fast. Madame de Sévigné told her daughter that the drink's supporters were as numerous as its opponents. When we examine the recipe books from the late seventeenth century, it turns out that the drink called "cocoa" (or "chocolate" by most French people) had more fat than the drink we know today. It also included cocoa butter, sugar, and sometimes hot milk (not to mention cream), and it is no wonder that those who drank it did not feel hunger for many hours.[2]

Cocoa arrived in England only in the mid-seventeenth century. We know that the drink was first sold in Oxford in 1650 and then

---

1   Madame de Sévigné's letters to her daughter are the basis of an interesting book by Nir Rachkovski, *Her Beloved Daughter* (Tel Aviv: Yedioth Books, 2013).

2   Details on how to prepare the drink can be found in the book *La Physiologie du Goût (The Physiology of Taste)* by gastronomer Brillat-Savarin (1755– 1826), which deals with food and drink. It was a highly regarded book for its time.

in London in 1657, where it was sold on Bishopsgate Street. The famous diary author, Pepys, mentions cocoa in November 1664, noting that it was sold in a café and was, he thought, very tasty. During the eighteenth century, cocoa was sold in London in cafés, and according to visitors from France it was a social fashion: The stylish society people who were called the "beau monde" would stroll in the mornings, and in the afternoons go to cafés to drink coffee or cocoa. The authors of the period, such as Joseph Addison (1672–1719) and Oliver Goldsmith (1728–1774), spent many hours in these cafés, along with major theater actors, such as David Garrick (1717–1779).

The cocoa merchants in England usually imported the cocoa beans, which did not have a customs duty, and ground them into powder. But they were supposed to pay a tax on every cup sold. Among the cocoa consumers was King George II. The production of cocoa powder was first centered in the city of Bristol, where factories to produce solid chocolate bars were later established. The leading names in chocolate production in England were Joseph Fry (1728–1787) and Dr. Hans Sloane (1660–1735), who produced fatty milk chocolate, which he believed was particularly healthy.

The Dutch chemist C. J. van Houten was mentioned earlier as the inventor of a machine separating cocoa butter fat from beans in 1828. Later on, it became clear that the public preferred the dry cocoa (made from cocoa powder). In 1842, Cadbury sold a thick milk chocolate bar, according to Sloane's recipe, and the product became popular. The largest UK chocolate producers—Cadbury, J. S. Fry, and Rowntree's—benefited from the growing demand. By the end of the century, solid chocolate became fashionable in the United States, and Milton Hershey (1857–1945) became a very wealthy man thanks to the chocolate he produced, which was perfectly suited to the public's taste. Thus the drink of the Aztec gods, and later the European nobility, became a drink suitable for all classes of people. As a solid product, chocolate is today a luxurious gift that can fit every budget.

5. A Little about Research

Like any plant, cocoa trees are susceptible to disease. Every year, there are epidemics that damage trees in one country or another, and at the same time, global demand for cocoa and chocolate is on the rise. There is a fear that in the near future there will be a shortage of chocolate and its price will rise. In order to avoid shortages, the solution is the crossbreeding of different varieties of cocoa to produce a tree more resistant to diseases. On this subject, experts follow precedents with other plants that have led to the development of resistant varieties (e.g., tomatoes, corn, and apples).

Like other cultivated fruits, cocoa trees also face a number of dangers. Among other things, there are diseases that are aggravated by the growers' tendency to grow only a few species that the public knows and loves. However, because of the limited gene pool, most species grown on a large scale are prone to the same diseases. In Costa Rica, where cocoa trees are grown, the authorities are aware of the problem. The cocoa industry in Costa Rica has had bitter experience, from a period in the 1980s when a white fungus called *Moniliophthora roreri*, Monilia, or "frosty pod rot" attacked the cocoa crops. The fungus accumulated on the pods and branches, and by the mid-1980s, there was a significant decline in the production of dried cocoa beans. To date, not all cocoa growers have managed to recover from that blow.

Even without the Monilia fungus, cocoa is considered a problematic crop. Often, due to various diseases, productivity decreases and profits fall. Costa Rica's project, with international backing, has dealt with this problem. In the early stages, the researchers focused on identifying the most resistant cocoa trees, which at the same time provide high yields. In the second stage, they began to hybridize different varieties in order to create new trees better and stronger than the previous ones. Growing hybrid plants is a lengthy process, and only after a dozen years or more can the research be determined to be a commercial success. Costa Rica has been a success. Some of the hybrid trees now produce three times the amount of cocoa as varieties grown in the past. The rate of Monilia fungus infection in hybrid varieties has dropped to 5 percent, compared to 75 percent in earlier varieties.

When I recently visited Costa Rica, hybrid cocoa varieties contributed greatly to farmers enjoying high productivity and survival from disease. At the same time, the improved trees need to produce good cocoa and tasty chocolate, and the research continues. Investigating consumer tastes is not a simple matter. Part of this is already discussed in the appendix to the wine chapter. The success of the hybrid varieties in Costa Rica encourages optimism for other agricultural products with similar problems. Suffice it to recall that three-quarters of the world's food comes from only twelve crops and four animal species. So our food supply is vulnerable to disease and pests. Annual crops that contract diseases can seriously damage the amount of available food in a given region. It happened in the mid-nineteenth century in Ireland and caused the death of hundreds of thousands. Today, it happens in other places, albeit in smaller dimensions.

Chapter Eleven

SOMETHING COLD TO DRINK?

1. The United States in the Last Century

Israeli author Ephraim Kishon has described a short culinary journey in the US in 1965. He relates that he went to a cafeteria in Washington, DC, and asked for "cold tea with no ice." He received tea with ice cubes, so he repeated his request for a "drink with no ice" in his precise Hungarian accent. Every time he requested they remove the ice, they added more ice cubes, until there was no room for tea in the large glass. It seems that in the United States, tea must be very cold, and there is no other option. There is a reason it's called "iced tea." My friend Rebel Cole chills the teapots in his home to almost zero degrees. Even today in the twenty-first century, we must drink cold, cold, cold tea. And now, with your permission, we will move from the modern West to the ancient East.

2. The Near East in Ancient Times

The kings of ancient Egypt, the pharaohs, loved chilled wine. There were no proper means for cooling beverages in Egypt, except perhaps a strong hail, such as the one Moses called for in the story of the plagues. Even today there is an occasional hailstorm, but it melts immediately and is certainly not suitable for cooling drinks. Wine was chilled by a method called "evaporative cooling." Wine in Egypt, as well as in Greece and Rome, was stored in clay jugs, which were kept in dry cellars during the day. At night, some of the jugs were moved to the roof of the palace. Each jug was placed in a tub of water, and household servants of the pharaoh would pour the water in a stream over the jugs. The night breeze would evaporate the water and thus cool the wine.

Neither the servants nor indeed the pharaoh himself understood exactly what was happening in the process of evaporative cooling, but the process worked well and in fact is still used in warm countries. Not only jugs of wine are cooled, entire mud huts are sprayed with water using sprinklers placed on the roof. This technique was also used in India, but there the cooled liquid was water. There are countries in Africa that use this method to this day.

Another liquid-cooling method was invented and perfected in ancient Persia. There they have high mountains covered with snow, and the snowmelt was used for cooling. Fields were irrigated using a system of underground channels of water called *qanats*. The channels were dug by teams of experts. After being dug, the qanats were covered with tamped earth and rock fragments, thus strengthening the channels and preventing dirt from getting into the flowing water from melting snow. The slope was calculated for a moderate flow of water, so that the channels would not be destroyed by a strong current. The wealthy used small clay water tanks to store the cold water that came from the channel, and they also chilled the water using evaporation. They built water "towers" on their rooftops that looked like chimneys with one side open to the night wind, which chilled the jugs of water in summer.

Excess water in ancient Persia was stored in water cisterns. Sometimes ice was also stored in the sealed cisterns, collected from artificial pools where the water froze in the winter. By the fifth century BCE, chunks of ice were stored in pits sealed with mortar mixed with straw. The water that dripped out when the ice melted was served to the household members in clay cups.

From time to time, the wealthy cistern owners would sell ice in the marketplace, which also helped the less wealthy residents to cool their milk and drinking water. It is important to mention that a surplus of cooked food could keep for a few days if it was cold. In the absence of refrigeration, excess food had to be salted. Water, as well as fruit juices, could be cooled. The word *sherbat* in ancient Persian describes sweet drinks based on fruit and spices. This is the origin of the word *sorbet,* which means chilled fruit juice. Even then you could dilute a sweet fruit syrup and enjoy a delicious beverage. Incidentally, this is a drink that is consumed today in Turkey, in the United States, and in Central Asia. The Persian cooling technology has been improved upon over hundreds of years. Alexander the Great visited Persia in the fourth century BCE and noted the advantages of storing winter snow for the hot summer days. His army transferred this cooling system to Greece and from there to Rome. Snow reserves that were filled in winter were also used in China and Japan, and Korean kings of the Joseon dynasty also enjoyed their benefits.

3. Chilling Drinks in Europe

The practice of using compressed snow to cool water was also well known in Europe. In the late Middle Ages, in Italian cities close to the Alps, snow was stored in a special room. The wealthy acquired packed snow used to cool drinks. Hampton Court Palace near London was built by Cardinal Woolsey (the chief minister of England) in 1514. It included a huge room for ice storage. King Charles II of England was an especially avid fan of cold drinks and built a majestic ice room in 1660. It was a huge facility, reviving ancient technology. The aristocracy of the seventeenth century established ice rooms filled with snow or ice in the winter that provided cold water in the early summer. They were usually built underground and accessed through a two-door underground passage to prevent infiltration of the summer heat.

Preserving ice from frozen winter puddles was common in other European countries, as well as in the US. US president George Washington wrote about the coolness of his "ice house" in 1785. Around that same time, Ottoman Turkish sultans were drinking fruit juices mixed with snow brought from the Uludağ Mountains near the city of Bursa, south of Istanbul. Indeed, it was not only the emperor of Rome, Nero, who enjoyed cold water from melting snow; the kings of Europe who followed him did so as well. As mentioned, cities near high mountains made cold water from snow, and in distant cities, such as London and Paris, ice was chilled in the winter and stored in underground ice rooms. This technology, of course, served only the high aristocracy. In the seventeenth and eighteenth centuries, there were harsh winters, and the "decorative" lakes in the estate gardens provided abundant ice.

For the wealthy around the world, this was an expensive solution for storing ice, but what about those with fewer resources? Here we have to mention the farmer Thomas Moore, who in 1802, invented an "icebox" that was used to transport butter from Maryland to the Washington, DC, markets. This icebox was a wooden box with an interior tin liner and covered with rabbit fur. Ice was placed between the wood and tin. In 1803 he patented his icebox, and then President Thomas Jefferson bought one for his personal use. There was not much demand for Thomas Moore's icebox. US residents continued to drink lukewarm water in their homes.

At the beginning of the nineteenth century, natural winter ice from shallow lakes in Massachusetts was transported in wagons and later on a train to be sold to interested buyers in Boston, New York, and Philadelphia. The American ice market attracted the attention of a young man, Frederic Tudor. He conceived a business plan that consisted of transporting ice on ships from Boston to the southern US states, to Cuba, and to other islands in the Caribbean Sea. The plan was simple. First, to obtain a monopoly on the sale of ice in the target markets. Second, to harvest ice from the Rockwood reservoir near Boston and load it on a ship. Third, to have the ship bring the ice to a target city (for example, to Havana, Cuba). Fourth, to sell the ice, get rich, and come back again the next year. The business logic was also simple: take a free product and transport it to a location where it commanded a high price. The problem was, the plan didn't work well. Tudor did not get rich. The long journey at sea created great depreciation, and in the target ports, people were not willing to pay such high prices for cold water. There were additional attempts, in the first quarter of the nineteenth century, to market American ice in Australia and India, but the logistical problems were great, and prices did not always cover the transportation costs.

4. Natural and Artificial Ice in the Nineteenth Century

Frederic Tudor did not get rich in the ice trade, but as early as the mid-nineteenth century, the ice business was gaining momentum in the United States. There was a slow but gradual climb in demand for ice to chill drinks, with a simultaneous growing demand within the industry. Ice was cut in the winter from shallow lakes in New England and stored in isolated warehouses, then transported (by blocks) to customers in the big eastern cities: New York, Boston, Philadelphia, and Washington, DC. At first, most of the buyers were drugstores selling cold soda water to the thirsty masses. In addition, coffee shops and restaurants that sold white wine and chilled Champagne began to buy ice. Soon, pubs followed suit by cooling the beer sold by putting beer barrels into tubs filled with ice cubes. As time went on, private customers joined in, so that they could chill food and drink in their own homes.

In the nineteenth century, there was a general belief in the United States that natural products were superior to artificial ones, and so natural ice, cut from frozen lakes in winter and kept in cold storage until the summer, was preferred. Even after physician John Snow discovered in 1849 that a cholera epidemic in London was caused by contaminated water from wells, the US still held a preference for natural ice. And indeed, the New England lakes provided beautiful, white ice that was delivered to the customers' homes and mixed with various kinds of drinks. Through Tudor's Ice Company and other companies, customers in the southern United States became accustomed to using natural ice transported by carriages. However, in the final decades of the nineteenth century there were several epidemics of typhus that were caused by melted natural ice.

At the same time, there were persistent attempts to produce artificial ice from pure water and transport it by rail to city centers. Artificial ice was sold mainly to households that had an ice box, also called a "refrigerator." It was a box with two compartments. A block of ice was placed in the top compartment, and the groceries were kept in the bottom compartment. As the ice melted, the water accumulated in a drawer at the bottom of the refrigerator. Every day, the drawer was emptied, and every few days, a new ice block was purchased. The iceboxes were not particularly effective, because the air that entered every time the door was opened caused the ice to melt faster.

The ice distribution system to customers was fairly efficient. Each supplier had a large ice warehouse near the railway station, and from there the ice was transported to customers in closed wagons.[1] The main problem was how to use steam power to make artificial ice.

In the early nineteenth century, inventor Oliver Evans formulated the principles of artificial cooling. During the following one hundred years, a cooling method was developed. The base was a liquid coolant called "refrigerant" that was enclosed in a closed loop, or coil. The system had a compressor and heat exchangers, which were basically additional tubes. The liquid entered the compressor as a gas that was compressed into a small volume and heated. It then moved from the compressor to the heat exchangers. From there, it emerged in the form of a cool liquid that cooled the surroundings. In other words, the liquid became a cool gas, and ice formed on the tube carrying it, which cooled the inside of the icebox.

Over the years, the cooling process was improved, and large cooling rooms were constructed, several stories high, that could produce cold water, cold beer, and cold soda for the public's enjoyment. At the same time, new cocktails were invented that suggested pouring alcohol and fruit juice onto ice. The general public recognized the need for ice cubes, which became a complementary product to many types of drinks. The use of iceboxes became popular. In 1903, French priest Marcel Audiffren invented

---

1   The delivery of blocks of ice to customers' homes was common in the US until the mid-twentieth century. Understandably, the distributors were muscular people who had to carry the blocks of ice to the entrance of the house. Joe Louis, world boxing champion from 1937–1949, delivered ice in Detroit before becoming a boxer.

the first household refrigerator. General Electric in the United States purchased the patent and as of 1911 sold household refrigerators for $1,000 each. That same year, an automobile cost $500. Various inventions and refinements have made the household refrigerator safe and convenient. One compartment is used as a freezer and for making homemade ice, and a second for food and drink. The leading application of refrigerators in the 1920s was the ability to produce ice cubes. In the United States, a "flavor revolution" began, and soft drinks were poured into glasses filled with ice cubes. Ever since then, it is very difficult to drink warm Coca-Cola.

Bibliography

General

Abulafia, D. *The New Cambridge Medieval History: 1098–1300.* Cambridge: Cambridge University Press, 1999.

Bober, P. P. *Art, Culture, and Cuisine: Ancient and Medieval Gastronomy.* Chicago: University of Chicago Press, 2001.

Braudel, F. *Civilization and Capitalism, 15th–18th Century: The Wheels of Commerce.* Volume 2. New York: Harper & Row Publishers, 1982.

Civitello, L. *Cuisine and Culture: A History of Food and People.* Hoboken, NJ: John Wiley & Sons, 2007.

Ferguson, N. *Empire: How Britain Made the Modern World.* London: Penguin UK, 2012.

Fernández-Armesto, F. *Food: A History.* London: Macmillan, 2001.

Levy, P. (ed.). *The Penguin Book of Food and Drink.* New York: Viking, Penguin Books, 1996.

Mintz, S. W. *Sweetness and Power: The Place of Sugar in Modern History.* New York: Viking, Penguin Books, 1985.

Mount, T. *Everyday Life in Medieval London.* Gloucestershire: Amberley Publishing, 2015.

Shiman, L. L. *Crusade Against Drink in Victorian England.* London: Macmillan, 1988.

Toussaint-Samat, M. *A History of Food.* Translated by Anthea Bell. Cambridge, MA: Wiley, 1994.

Standage, T. *An Edible History of Humanity*. New York: Walker & Co., 2009.

Strong, R. *Feast: A History of Grand Eating*. Orlando and Austin: Harcourt Inc., 2002.

Chapter One: All Who Are Thirsty, Come to the Waters

Cohen, M. N. *Health and the Rise of Civilization*. New Haven: Yale University Press, 1989.

Chadwick, E. *Report on the Sanitary Condition of the Labouring Population in Great Britain*. Edinburgh: Edinburgh University Press, 1965. First published 1842.

Goubert, J-P. *The Conquest of Water: The Advent of Health in the Industrial Age*. Translated by H. Wilson. Cambridge: Polity Press, 1989.

Hamlin, C. *A Science of Impurity: Water Analysis in Nineteenth Century Britain*. Berkeley: University of California Press, 1990.

Chapter Two: Wine That Gladdens Human Hearts

Hopfer, H., and H. Heymann, "Judging Wine Quality: Do We Need Experts, Consumers or Trained Panelists?" *Food Quality and Preference*, 32 (2014): 221–233.

McGovern, P. E., S. J. Fleming, and S. H. Katz (eds.). *The Origins and Ancient History of Wine: Food and Nutrition in History and Anthropology*. London: Routledge, 2003.

Nygren, I., E. Gustavson, and L. Johnson. "Perceived Flavour Changes in Blue Mould Cheese After Tasting White Wine." *Food Service Technology*, 3 (2003): 143–150.

Paulson, M., G. Rogusa, and M. Hersleth. "Consumer Perception of Food-Beverage Pairing." *International Journal of Gastronomy and Food Science*, 2 (2015): 83–92.

Phillips, R. *A Short History of Wine*. London: Penguin Books, 2001.

Robinson, J. (ed.). *The Oxford Companion to Wine*. Oxford University Press UK, 2006.

Thomas, A., M. Viaslli, E. Cordelle, and P. Schlich. "Temporal Drivers of Liking." *Food Quality and Preference*, 40 (2015): 365–375.

kosherwinesociety.com.

http://www.religiousrules.com/Judaismfood00table.htm

Chapter Three: Beer Is Everywhere

Harari, Yuval Noah. *Sapiens: A Brief History of Humankind* (Hebrew). Tel Aviv-Yafo: Kinneret Zmora Bitan Dvir, 2011.

Kramer, S. N. *History Begins at Sumer*. London: Themes & Hudson, 1961.

Trigger, B. G. *Understanding Early Civilizations: A Comparative Study*. Cambridge: Cambridge University Press, 2003.

Chapter Four: Alcohol—the Beverage of Life

Braun, S. *Buzz: The Science and Lore of Alcohol and Caffeine*. Oxford: Oxford University Press, 1996.

Camporesi, P. *Exotic Brew: The Art of Living in the Age of Enlightenment*. Translated by C. Woodall. Oxford: Polity Press, 1994.

Heath, D. B. *Drinking Occasions: Comparative Perspectives on Alcohol and Culture*. Oxford, Psychology Press, 2000.

National Institutes of Health. *NESARC—Survey on Alcohol and Related Conditions*. Washington, DC, 2006.

Regan, G. *The Joy of Mixology: The Consummate Guide to the Bartender's Craft*. New York: Clarkson Potter, 2003.

Sournia, J-C. *A History of Alcoholism*. Oxford: Basil Blackwell, 1990.

Thomas, J. *Jerry Thomas Bartenders Guide: How to Mix All Kinds of Plain and Fancy Drinks*. Dover, 2016. First published in 1862.

Wondrich, D. *Imbibe!: From Absinthe Cocktail to Whiskey Smash, a Salute in Stories and Drinks to "Professor" Jerry Thomas, Pioneer of the American Bar Featuring the Original Formulae*. New York: Penguin Books, 2007.

Chapter Five: The Main Types of Alcoholic Beverages

Cheever, S. *Drinking in America: Our Secret History*. New York: Grand Central Publishing, 2015.

Hundert, Gershon David. *Jews in Poland-Lithuania in the Eighteenth Century*. Berkeley: University of California Press, 2004.

Pack, A. J. *Nelson's Blood: The Story of Naval Rum*. Annapolis: US Naval Institute Press, 1996.

Rudgley, R. *Essential Substances: A Cultural History of Intoxicants in Society*. New York: Kodansha International, 1993.

Thompson, P. *Rum Punch and Revolution*. Philadelphia: University of Pennsylvania Press, 1999.

www.hachettebookgroup.com/titles/Susan.

Chapter Six: Tea (and Rice) in China and India

Berg, M. *Luxury and Pleasure in Eighteenth-Century Britain*. Oxford: Oxford University Press, 2005.

Davis, R. *The Industrial Revolution and British Overseas Trade*. Leicester: Leicester University Press, 1979.

Farrington, A. *Trading Places: The East India Company and Asia 1600–1834*. London: British Library Board, 2002.

Forrest, D. *Tea for the British: The Social and Economic History of a Famous Trade*. London: Chatto & Windus, 1973.

James, L. *The Rise and Fall of the British Empire*. London: Macmillan, 1994.

Macfarlane, A., and I. Macfarlane. *Green Gold: The Empire of Tea*. New York: Random House, 2011.

Tuchman B. W. *The March of Folly: From Troy to Vietnam*. New York: Ballentine Books, 1984.

Ukers, W. H. *All About Tea*. New York: The Tea and Coffee Trade Journal Company, 1922.

Wild, A. *The East India Company: Trade and Conquest from 1600*. New York: Harper Collins Illustrated, 2000.

Chapter Seven: Coffee, Wakefulness and Enlightenment

Cowan, B. *The Social Life of Coffee: The Emergence of the British Coffee House*. New Haven: Yale University Press, 2005.

Efron, J. *Medicine and the German Jews: A History*. New Haven: Yale University Press, 2001.

Endelman, T. *The Jews of Georgian England*. Philadelphia: Jewish Publication Society, 1979.

Feiner, S. *The Origins of Jewish Secularization in Eighteenth-Century Europe*. Jerusalem: Shazar Center, 2010.

Hattox, R. S. *Coffee and Coffeehouses: The Origins of a Social Beverage in the Medieval Near East*. Seattle: University of Washington Press, 2014.

Hess, J. *German Jews and the Claims of Modernity*. New Haven: Yale University Press, 2002.

Hundert, Gershon David. *Jews in Poland-Lithuania in the Eighteenth Century*. Berkeley and Los Angeles: University of California Press, 2004.

Liberles, R. *Jews Welcome Coffee: Tradition and Innovation in Early Modern Germany* (Hebrew). Jerusalem: Carmel, 2016.

Liss, D. *The Coffee Trader*. New York: Random House, 2003.

Ukers, W. H. *All About Coffee*. New York: The Tea and Coffee Trade Journal Company, 1922.

http://www.NCAUSA.org/ABOUT-COFFEE.

http://www.hilinecoffee.com/blog/types-of-coffee-roast.

Chapter Eight: Soft Drinks

Dietz, L. *Soda Pop: The History, Advertising, Art and Memorabilia of Soft Drinks in America*. New York: Simon & Schuster, 1973.

Emmins, C. *Soft Drinks: Their Origins and History*. Buckinghamshire: Shire Publication, 1991.

Hays, C. *Pop: Truth and Power at the Coca-Cola Company*. New York: Random House, 2010.

Pendergrast, M. *For God, Country and Coca-Cola: The Unauthorized History of the World's Most Popular Soft Drink*. London: Orion Books, 1994.

Standage, T. *A History of the World in 6 Glasses*. New York: Bloomsbury, 2005.

Chapter Nine: Milk (and Honey)

Australian Dairy Corporation. *Push for Freer World Dairy Trade Statement*, 2000.

Boyazoglu, J., I. Hatziminaoglu, and P. Morand-Fehr. "The Role of the Goat in Society: Past, Present and Perspectives for the Future." *Small Ruminant Research* 60, issues 1–2 (2005): 13–23.

Boynton, R. D. *Milk Marketing in California*. Sacramento, CA: Dairy Institute of California, 1992.

Cardwell, M. *Milk Quota—European Community and United Kingdom Law*. Oxford: Clarendon Press, 1996.

Darby, W. J., P. Ghalioungui, and L. Grivetti. *Food: The Gift of Osiris*. London: Academic Press, 1977.

Dory, S. *News from the Past: Chapters from the History of Dairy in Israel*. Caesarea: Cattle-growers Association (Hebrew), 1996.

Fussel, G. E. *The English Dairy Farmer, 1500–1900*. London: Frank Cass, 1966.

Goitein, S. D. *A Mediterranean Society*. Volume 1. Berkeley and Los Angeles: University of California Press, 1967.

Goitein, S. D. *Letters of Medieval Jewish Traders*. Princeton: Princeton University Press, 1973.

Hart, S. P. "Recent Perspectives in Using Goats for Vegetation Management in the USA." *Journal of Dairy Science* 48 (2001): 170–176.

Lane, F. C. *Venice and History*. Baltimore: Johns Hopkins University Press, 1966.

Morand-Fehr, P. "Capacité D'adaptation des Chevre en Milieu Difficile." *Ethnozootechnie* 41 (1988): 63–86.

Nissen, H. J., P. Damero, and R. K. Englund. *Archaic Bookkeeping*. Translated by P. Larsen. Chicago: Chicago University Press, 1993.

Trotman, C. *The Development of Milk Quotas in the U.K.* London: Sweet & Maxwell Ltd., 1996.

Valenze, D. *Milk: A Local and Global History*. New Haven: Yale University Press, 2011.

www.dairy.com.au/news.

http://www.historylearningsite.co.uk/a-history-of-medicine/louis-pasteur.

Chapter Ten: Cocoa—The Drink of Nobility

Barr, A. *Drink: A Social History*. London: Pimlico, 1998.

Brenner, J. G. *The Chocolate Wars: Inside the Secret World of Mars and Hershey*. London: HarperCollins, 1999.

Christie, A. *The Mysterious Affair at Styles*. New York: John Lane, 1920.

Clarence-Smith, W. G. *Cocoa and Chocolate, 1765–1914*. London and New York: Routledge, 2000.

Coe, S. D., and M. D. Coe. *The True History of Chocolate*. London: Thames & Hudson, 1996.

Dand, R. *The International Cocoa Trade*. Cambridge: Woodhead, 1993.

Mintz, S. W. *Sweetness and Power*. New York: Viking, 1985.

Rachkovsky, N. *Beloved Daughter* (Hebrew). Tel Aviv: Yediot, 2013.

Rubinstein, H. *The Chocolate Book*. London: Penguin Books, 1982.

Wagner, G. *The Chocolate Conscience*. London: Chatto & Windus, 1987.

Young, A. M. *The Chocolate Tree: A Natural History of Cacao*. Washington, DC: Smithsonian Institute Press, 1994.

Chapter Eleven: Something Cold to Drink?

Freidberg, S. *Fresh: A Perishable History*. Cambridge, MA: Harvard University Press, 2009.

Jackson, T. *Chilled: How Refrigeration Changed the World and Might Do So Again*. London: Bloomsbury Publishing Plc., 2015.

Kishon E. *Somersaults* (Hebrew). Tel Aviv: Teversky Press (1965): 227.

Rees, J. *Refrigeration Nations: A History of Ice, Appliances, and Enterprise in America.* Baltimore: Johns Hopkins University Press, 2013.

Shachtman, T. *Absolute Zero and the Conquest of Cold.* New York: Mariner Books, 2000.

About the Author

Arie L. Melnik is Professor Emeritus of Finance and Economics at the University of Haifa. He received his M.Sc. and Ph.D. from Cornell University (U.S.). In the past he taught at Michigan State University (U.S.), Northwestern University (U.S.), York University (Canada), University of California, Berkeley (U.S.), New York University (U.S.),  City University Business School (London, U.K.), and UNSW (Sydney, Australia). Melnik's major areas of interest are Financial Economics and Economic History. He has contributed to major academic journals.

In addition to academic work, Arie Melnik occupied several civic and business positions. He was a member of the Council for Higher Education. In addition, he was a board member of Bank Leumi. He was also a member of the board of directors of Rambam Medical Center. At present he is a member of the board of directors of Maccabi Health Services (second largest HMO in Israel).